Prisoner for God

LETTERS AND PAPERS FROM PRISON

BY DIETRICH BONHOEFFER
The Cost of Discipleship
Prisoner for God: Letters and Papers from Prison

Prisoner for God

LETTERS AND PAPERS FROM PRISON

by

DIETRICH BONHOEFFER

EDITED BY EBERHARD BETHGE

TRANSLATED BY REGINALD H. FULLER

New York   The Macmillan Company   1954

The original edition of this book was published in Germany under the title *Widerstand und Ergebung—Briefe
und Aufzeichnungen aus der Haft,* by Chr. Kaiser
Verlag, München, Germany.

Published in England under the title *Letters and
Papers from Prison.*

Contents

Editor's Foreword

DIETRICH BONHOEFFER's father was a great doctor, a psychiatrist teaching at Berlin University; his forebears included mayors and parsons. In Schwäbisch-Hall in Württemberg there are old tombstones in the church bearing the name of Bonhoeffer. His mother was a grand-daughter of Karl von Hase. He was a well-known Professor of Church History in Jena and he too had a taste of imprisonment in a fortress, a result of his zeal for the freedom of student corporations.

It was with such a background that Dietrich Bonhoeffer grew up as a member of a large family (he was born on 14th February 1906 in Breslau). In Berlin-Grunewald he played with the children of Adolf von Harnack, the universal theologian, and of Hans Delbrück, the well-known historian. In the summer of 1924 he commenced his studies at Berlin University, was made a licentiate in 1927 with a thesis on *Communio Sanctorum*. Though Harnack, Seeberg and Lietzmann, the most influential teachers in Berlin, thought very highly of the accomplished young theologian, he came more and more under the influence of Karl Barth, whom he had not yet heard lecturing. This influence is clearly seen in his later University thesis, *Akt und Sein*, in which he clearly acknowledges the importance of dialectical theology for the history of philosophy and theology.

After a brief period as pastor in Barcelona (1928-9), and a year of study at Union Theological Seminary, New York (1930), he commenced teaching in Berlin, where he continued, with some intervals, until finally forbidden to teach by the National-Socialist authorities in 1936. The most significant break in these years occurred when he took charge of the German congregations of St. Paul and Sydenham in London from 1933-5. The reason for this step was to make an unequivocal protest against the incipient taint of the 'German Christians' in the Church in Germany. From this time he became one of the most important interpreters of German events for the ecumenical Church in the West.

While he was preparing, in contact with C. F. Andrews, for a visit to Gandhi, he received a call from the Confessing Church in Germany to return home in order to lead an emergency Seminary in Pomerania for young ministers. It was in this task that Bonhoeffer's theological and personal influence was at its greatest. Here he wrote the tracts against compromise in the Church struggle. Here *The Cost of Discipleship* was written (1937), as well as *Gemeinsames Leben* (1938)— the two works which during his lifetime made his name and his thoughts most widely known.

While the discussion about his stirring attack on 'cheap grace' in *The Cost of Discipleship* was still proceeding, developments of a quite different kind were beginning to change the whole direction of his life and his thought. Through his brother-in-law Hans von Dohnanyi he was able to have a glimpse behind the scenes of the crisis which centred on General von Fritsch, and of the plans for overthrowing the Nazi government which were associated with General Beck. Hitherto Bonhoeffer, under the influence of his American and English experiences, had been very near to absolute pacifism— an unheard-of position in the Germany of that time. Now he began to see pacifism as an illegitimate escape, especially if he was tempted to withdraw from his increasing contacts with the responsible political and military leaders of the resistance. He no longer saw any way of escape into some region of piety. In 1939, when in the course of a lecture tour in America, he was pressed on every hand by his American friends to stay in America and there to take up some task suitable to his ecumenical spirit and his fine sensitivity to church life in other lands, he resolved to return to Germany, into what was clearly a deteriorating situation, and he took one of the last ships sailing back to Germany before the war. In his Diary he writes, 'I do not understand why I am here. . . . The short prayer in which we thought of our German brothers, almost overwhelmed me. . . . If matters become more uncertain I shall certainly return to Germany. . . . In the event of war I shall not stay in America . . .' and finally, 'Since coming on board ship my inner disruption about the future has disappeared.'

Now began a life spent between the tasks of the Confessing Church, visitation, and his work at the great task of his *Ethics*, which finally appeared posthumously and unfinished in 1949; together with the tasks of the Resistance movement, with all its journeyings. Among these, and the most difficult and moving of all, was a visit to Stockholm in 1942, in order to have conversations with the Bishop of Chichester. On the one hand he had his church work with all the obstacles set in his way by the Gestapo—forbidden to lecture, to write, or to make speeches of any kind, and forbidden to remain in Berlin; and on the other hand he was provided quietly with all the passes and papers which a privileged courier needed. Extraordinary confidence was thus placed in him; but it did not last. One bright Monday in April 1943 we heard that Hans von Dohnanyi had been arrested in his office, and we waited for the motor-car to draw up before Bonhoeffer's door. We made the room as ready for the expected visit as we could: documents were placed in safety, and others were laid on the table —which might provide misleading and unimportant information. Matters took their expected course, and Bonhoeffer was arrested.

Dietrich Bonhoeffer spent the first eighteen months of his confinement in the military section of Tegel Prison in Berlin. This was from April 5th 1943 until October 8th 1944. After a certain amount of quibbling he was given permission to write to his parents. The first part of this book consists of selections from the letters he wrote to them. They had to pass through the prison censorship, and in particular they were read by Dr. Roeder, who was in charge of judicial examinations. This circumstance has naturally affected their contents. More obvious however is Bonhoeffer's concern to allay the anxieties of his family.

In six months, however, Bonhoeffer had made such good friends among the warders and medical orderlies that he was able to embark upon an extensive correspondence, partly by letter, partly on scraps of paper. This correspondence was addressed to a number of friends, including the present editor. It was only necessary to observe certain rules for the sake of security. Thus, communications about certain persons in dangerous positions, about the progress of the resistance movement and about the investigations into his own case had to be made in code. But the correspondence proceeded without interruption until the stringent measures consequent upon July 20th,[1] and the discovery of the Zossen papers (documents, diaries and other incriminating evidence relating to the members of the resistance movement associated with Canaris, Oster, Hans von Dohnanyi and others) in September 1944. As a consequence Bonhoeffer was removed by the Gestapo to close confinement in Prinz Albert Strasse. Unfortunately this move, together with the arrest of the editor in October 1944, necessitated the destruction, for security reasons, of the letters written during the last months at Tegel. All the earlier letters had been deposited in a safe resting-place. These letters form the second part of this volume. In these Bonhoeffer speaks freely of his experiences, thoughts and emotions, unhampered by the inquisitive eye of strangers.

With the letters he sent me he enclosed some of his written work, consisting of prayers, poems and reflections.

These letters enable us to reconstruct the picture of life in a prison cell as it was lived by a man of extraordinary sensitivity. Here we can see the intimate details of an individual life fused into a striking unity with the disastrous events which were going on in the world outside, a unity produced by a reflective mind and a sensitive heart. The whole picture is given a devastating summary in the brief letter of July 21st 1944 and in the 'Stations on the Road to Freedom', composed after the news of the failure of July 20th at a time when Bonhoeffer became convinced that his end was near. The failure of the plot was a dreadful blow for Bonhoeffer, but he met it with renewed dedication to the service of his people and with steadfast determination to bear all the consequences and the additional

[1] The date of the unsuccessful attempt on Hitler's life. (*Translator.*)

pain. In time to come it will be better appreciated how this second act of dedication justifies the first and sealed it as an undying heritage. This heritage may lie dormant, but it can never be lost.

In the Prinz Albert Strasse opportunities of contact were much reduced. The acceptance and despatch of messages or the necessities of life depended entirely on the caprice of the commissars. One day Dietrich's family found that he had disappeared. The Gestapo absolutely refused to give any information as to his whereabouts. That was in February. It was not until the summer of 1945, some time after the collapse of Germany, that we learnt what had happened to him. He had been removed first to Buchenwald, then to Schönberg, and finally to Flossenbürg. And now the circumstances of his end are gradually coming to light. The letters from prison are preceded by an essay entitled 'After Ten Years'. This was composed at the turn of the year, 1942-3, and sent to a few friends as a Christmas present. At that time warnings had already been received, chiefly by Hans von Dohnyani, that the Central Bureau for the Security of the Reich was collecting evidence against Bonhoeffer and was bent on his arrest. This fragmentary essay was stowed away among the beams and rafters, where it survived the attentions of the police and enemy bombs. It is a testimony to the spirit in which we lived at the time and, if need arose, suffered too.

Bonhoeffer's last weeks were spent with prisoners drawn from all over Europe. Among them was Payne Best, an English officer. In his book *The Venlo Incident* Best writes: 'Bonhoeffer . . . was all humility and sweetness, he always seemed to me to diffuse an atmosphere of happiness, of joy in every smallest event in life, and of deep gratitude for the mere fact that he was alive. . . . He was one of the very few men that I have ever met to whom his God was real and close to him.'[1] And again, 'The following day, Sunday 8th April, 1945, Pastor Bonhoeffer held a little service and spoke to us in a manner which reached the hearts of all, finding just the right words to express the spirit of our imprisonment and the

[1] p. 180.

thoughts and resolutions which it had brought. He had hardly finished his last prayer when the door opened and two evil-looking men in civilian clothes came in and said: "Prisoner Bonhoeffer, get ready to come with us." Those words "come with us"—for all prisoners they had come to mean one thing only—the scaffold.

'We bade him good-bye—he drew me aside—"This is the end," he said. "For me the beginning of life," and then he gave me a message to give, if I could, to the Bishop of Chichester. . . . Next day, at Flossenbürg, he was hanged.'

This was in Schönberg, a little village in the Bavarian forest. A school classroom was his last halting-place, and men of every land of Europe and of once hostile confessions his last companions on earth.

EBERHARD BETHGE

Acknowledgments are due to Mr. J. B. Leishman for the English version of the poem on p. 165, and to Mr. Geoffrey Winthrop Young for the poems on pp. 151, 167 and 187.

I

After Ten Years

TEN YEARS is a long stretch in a man's life. Time is the most precious gift in our possession, for it is the most irrevocable. This is what makes it so disturbing to look back upon time we have lost. Time lost is time when we have not lived a full ✓ human life, time unenriched by experience, creative endeavour, enjoyment and suffering. Time lost is time we have not filled, time left empty. The past ten years have not been like that. Our losses have been immeasurable, but we have not lost time. True, knowledge and experience, which are realized only in retrospect, are mere abstractions compared with the reality, compared with the life we have actually lived. But just as the capacity to forget is a gift of grace, so memory, the recalling of the lessons we have learnt, is an essential element in responsible living. In the following pages I hope to put on record some of the lessons we have learnt and the experiences we have shared during the past ten years. These are not just individual experiences; they are not arranged in an orderly way, there is no attempt to discuss them or to theorize about them. All I have done is to jot down as they come some of the discoveries made by a circle of like-minded friends, discoveries about the business of human life. The only connexion between them is that of concrete experience. There is nothing new or startling about them, for they have been known long before. But to us has been granted the privilege of learning them anew by first-hand experience. I cannot write a single word about these things without a deep sense of gratitude for the fellowship of spirit and community of life we have been allowed to enjoy and preserve throughout these years.

No Ground beneath our Feet

Surely there has never been a generation in the course of human history with so little ground under its feet as our own.

Every conceivable alternative seems equally intolerable. We try to escape from the present by looking entirely to the past or the future for our inspiration, and yet, without indulging in fanciful dreams, we are able to wait for the success of our cause in quietness and confidence. It may be however that the responsible, thinking people of earlier generations who stood at a turning-point of history felt just as we do, for the very reason that something new was being born which was not discernible in the alternatives of the present.

Who Stands his Ground?

The great masquerade of evil has wrought havoc with all our ethical preconceptions. This appearance of evil in the guise of light, beneficence and historical necessity is utterly bewildering to anyone nurtured in our traditional ethical systems. But for the Christian who frames his life on the Bible it simply confirms the radical evilness of evil.

The failure of rationalism is evident. With the best of intentions, but with a naïve lack of realism, the rationalist imagines that a small dose of reason will be enough to put the world right. In his short-sightedness he wants to do justice to all sides, but in the mêlée of conflicting forces he gets trampled upon without having achieved the slightest effect. Disappointed by the irrationality of the world, he realizes at last his futility, retires from the fray, and weakly surrenders to the winning side.

Worse still is the total collapse of moral fanaticism. The fanatic imagines that his moral purity will prove a match for the power of evil, but like a bull he goes for the red rag instead of the man who carries it, grows weary and succumbs. He becomes entangled with non-essentials and falls into the trap set by the superior ingenuity of his adversary.

Then there is the man with a conscience. He fights single-handed against overwhelming odds in situations which demand a decision. But there are so many conflicts going on, all of which demand some vital choice—with no advice or support save that of his own conscience—that he is torn to pieces.

[14

Evil approaches him in so many specious and deceptive guises that his conscience becomes nervous and vacillating. In the end he contents himself with a salved instead of a clear conscience, and starts lying to his conscience as a means of avoiding despair. If a man relies exclusively on his conscience he fails to see how a bad conscience is sometimes more wholesome and strong than a deluded one.

When men are confronted by a bewildering variety of alternatives, the path of *duty* seems to offer a sure way out. They grasp at the imperative as the one certainty. The responsibility for the imperative rests upon its author, not upon its executor. But when men are confined to the limits of duty, they never risk a daring deed on their own responsibility, which is the only way to score a bull's eye against evil and defeat it. The man of duty will in the end be forced to give the devil his due.

What then of the man of *freedom*? He is the man who aspires to stand his ground in the world, who values the necessary deed more highly than a clear conscience or the duties of his calling, who is ready to sacrifice a barren principle for a fruitful compromise or a barren mediocrity for a fruitful radicalism. What then of him? He must beware lest his freedom should become his own undoing. For in choosing the lesser of two evils he may fail to see that the greater evil he seeks to avoid may prove the lesser. Here we have the raw material of tragedy.

Some seek refuge from the rough-and-tumble of public life in the sanctuary of their own private virtue. Such men however are compelled to seal their lips and shut their eyes to the injustice around them. Only at the cost of self-deception can they keep themselves pure from the defilements incurred by responsible action. For all that they achieve, that which they leave undone will still torment their peace of mind. They will either go to pieces in face of this disquiet, or develop into the most hypocritical of all Pharisees.

Who stands his ground? Only the man whose ultimate criterion is not in his reason, his principles, his conscience, his freedom or his virtue, but who is ready to sacrifice all these

15]

things when he is called to obedient and responsible action in faith and exclusive allegiance to God. The responsible man seeks to make his whole life a response to the question and call of God.

Civil Courage?

What lies behind the complaint about the dearth of civil courage? The last ten years have produced a rich harvest of bravery and self-sacrifice, but hardly any civil courage, even among ourselves. To attribute this to personal cowardice would be an all too facile psychology. Its background must be sought elsewhere. In the course of a long history we Germans have had to learn the necessity and the power of obedience. The subordination of all individual desires and opinions to the call of duty has given meaning and nobility to life. We have looked upwards, not in servile fear, but in free trust, seeing our duty as a call, and the call as a vocation. This readiness to follow a command from above rather than our own private opinion of what was best was a sign of a legitimate self-distrust. Who can deny that in obedience, duty and calling we Germans have again and again excelled in bravery and self-sacrifice? But the German has preserved his freedom—what nation has talked so passionately of freedom as we have, from Luther to the idealists?—by seeking deliverance from his own will through service to the community. Calling and freedom were two sides of the same thing. The trouble was, he did not understand his world. He forgot that submissiveness and self-sacrifice could be exploited for evil ends. Once that happened, once the exercise of the calling itself became questionable, all the ideals of the German would begin to totter. Inevitably he was convicted of a fundamental failure: he could not see that in certain circumstances free and responsible action might have to take precedence over duty and calling. As a compensation he developed in one direction an irresponsible unscrupulousness, and in another an agonising scrupulosity which invariably frustrated action. Civil courage however can only grow out of the free responsibility of free men. Only

[16

now are we Germans beginning to discover the meaning of free responsibility. It depends upon a God who demands bold action as the free response of faith, and who promises forgiveness and consolation to the man who becomes a sinner in the process.

Rationaliz.?
Spirit?

Of Success

Though success can never justify an evil deed or the use of questionable means, it is not an ethically neutral thing. All the same it remains true that historical success creates the only basis for the continuance of life, and it is still a moot point whether it is ethically more responsible to behave like Don Quixote and enter the lists against a new age, or to admit one's defeat, accept the new age and agree to serve it. In the last resort success makes history, and the Disposer of history is always bringing good out of evil over the heads of the history-makers. To ignore the ethical significance of success is to betray a superficial acquaintance with history and a defective sense of responsibility. So it is all to the good that we have been forced for once to grapple seriously with this problem of the ethics of success. All the time goodness is successful we can afford the luxury of regarding success as having no ethical significance. But the problem arises when success is achieved by evil means. It is no good then behaving as an arm-chair critic and disputing the issue, for that is to refuse to face the facts. Nor is opportunism any help, for that is to capitulate before success. We must be determined not to be outraged critics or mere opportunists. We must take our full share of responsibility for the moulding of history, whether it be as victors or vanquished. It is only by refusing to allow any event to deprive us of our responsibility for history, because we know that is a responsibility laid upon us by God, that we shall achieve a relation to the events of history far more fruitful than criticism or opportunism. To talk about going down fighting like heroes in face of certain defeat is not really heroic at all, but a failure to face up to the future. The ultimate question the man of responsibility asks is not, How can I extricate myself heroically from the affair? but, How is the coming generation to live? It is only in this way that fruitful solutions can arise, even if for the time being they are humiliating. In short it is easier by far to act on abstract principle than from concrete responsibility. The rising generation will always instinctively discern which of the two we are acting upon. For it is their future which is at stake.

Of Folly

Folly is a more dangerous enemy to the good than malice. You can protest against malice, you can unmask it or prevent it by force. Malice always contains the seeds of its own destruction, for it always makes men uncomfortable, if nothing worse. There is no defence against folly. Neither protests nor force are of any avail against it, and it is never amenable to reason. If facts contradict personal prejudices, there is no need to believe them, and if they are undeniable, they can simply be pushed aside as exceptions. Thus the fool, as compared with the scoundrel, is invariably self-complacent. And he can easily become dangerous, for it does not take much to make him aggressive. Hence folly requires much more cautious handling than malice. We shall never again try to reason with the fool, for it is both useless and dangerous.

To deal adequately with folly it is essential to recognize it for what it is. This much is certain, it is a moral rather than an intellectual defect. There are men of great intellect who are fools, and men of low intellect who are anything but fools, a discovery we make to our surprise as a result of particular circumstances. The impression we derive is that folly is acquired rather than congenital; it is acquired in certain circumstances where men make fools of themselves or allow others to make fools of them. We observe further that folly is less common in the unsociable or the solitary than in individuals or groups who are inclined or condemned to sociability. From this it would appear that folly is a sociological problem rather than one of psychology. It is a special form of the operation of historical circumstances upon men, a psychological by-product of definite external factors. On closer inspection it would seem that any violent revolution, whether political or religious, produces an outburst of folly in a large part of mankind. Indeed, it would seem to be almost a law of psychology and sociology. The power of one needs the folly of the other. It is not that certain aptitudes of men, intellectual aptitudes for instance, become stunted or destroyed. Rather, the upsurge of power is so terrific that it deprives men of an independent judgement, and they give up trying—more or less unconsciously—to assess the new state of affairs for themselves. The fool can often be stubborn, but this must not mislead us into thinking he is independent. One feels somehow, especially in conversation with him, that it is impossible to talk to the man himself, to talk to him personally. Instead, one is confronted with a series of slogans, watchwords, and the like, which have acquired power over him. He is under a curse, he is blinded, his very humanity is being prostituted and exploited. Once he has surrendered his will and become a mere tool, there are no lengths of evil to which the fool will not go, yet all the time he is unable to see that it is evil. Here lies the danger of a diabolical exploitation of humanity, which can do irreparable damage to the human character.

But it is just at this point that we realize that the fool cannot be saved by education. What he needs is redemption. There is nothing else for it. Until then it is no earthly good trying to convince him by rational argument. In this state of affairs we can well understand why it is no use trying to find out what 'the people' really think, and why this question is also so superfluous for the man who thinks and acts responsibly. As the Bible says, 'the fear of the Lord is the beginning of wisdom'. In other words, the only cure for folly is spiritual redemption, for that alone can enable a man to live as a responsible person in the sight of God.

But there is a grain of consolation in these reflections on human folly. There is no reason for us to think that the majority of men are fools under all circumstances. What matters in the long run is whether our rulers hope to gain more from the folly of men, or from their independence of judgement and their shrewdness of mind.

Contempt for Humanity?

There is a very real danger of our drifting into an attitude of contempt for humanity. We know full well that it would be very wrong, and that it would lead to a sterile relationship with our fellow men. Perhaps the following considerations will save us from this temptation. The trouble about it is that it lands us into the worst mistake of our enemies. The man who despises others can never hope to do anything with them. The faults we despise in others are always, to some extent at least, our own too. How often have we expected from others more than we are prepared to do ourselves! Why have we until now held such lofty views about human nature? Why have we not recognized its frailty and liability to temptation? We must form our estimate of men less from their achievements and failures, and more from their sufferings. The only profitable relationship to others—and especially to our weaker brethren—is one of love, that is the will to hold fellowship with them. Even God did not despise humanity, but became Man for man's sake.

Immanent Righteousness

It is one of the most astounding discoveries, but one of the most incontrovertible, that evil—often in a surprisingly short time—proves its own folly and defeats its own object. That is not to say that every evil deed is at once followed automatically by retribution. But it does mean that the deliberate transgression of the divine law on the plea of self-preservation has the opposite effect of self-destruction. This is something we have learnt from our own experience, and it can be interpreted in various ways. But one certain conclusion we can draw from it seems to be that social life is governed by certain laws more powerful than any other factors which may claim to be determinative. Hence it is not only unjust, but positively unwise to ignore these laws. Perhaps that is why Aristotle and St. Thomas Aquinas made prudence one of the cardinal virtues. Prudence and folly are not ethical *adiaphora*, as some

[20

Neo-protestant and *Gesinnungs*-ethics have tried to make out. The prudent man sees not only the possibilities of every concrete situation, but also the limits to human behaviour which are set by the eternal laws of social life. The prudent man acts virtuously and the virtuous man prudently.

It is true that all great historical action is constantly disregarding these laws. But it makes all the difference in the world whether it does so on principle, as though it contained a justification of its own, or whether it is still realized that to break these laws is sin, even if it be unavoidable, and that it can only be justified if the law is at once re-instated and respected. It is not necessarily hypocrisy when the declared aim of political action is the restoration of the law and not just blatant self-preservation. The world *is* simply ordered in such a way that a profound respect for the absolute laws and human rights is also the best means of self-preservation. While these laws may on occasion be broken in case of necessity, to proclaim that necessity as a principle and to take the law into our own hands is bound to bring retribution sooner or later. The immanent righteousness of history only rewards and punishes the deeds of men, the eternal righteousness of God tries and judges their hearts.

A Few Articles of Faith on the Sovereignty of God in History

I believe that God both can and will bring good out of evil. For that purpose he needs men who make the best use of everything. I believe God will give us all the power we need to resist in all time of distress. But he never gives it in advance, lest we should rely upon ourselves and not on him alone. A faith as strong as this should allay all our fears for the future. I believe that even our errors and mistakes are turned to good account. It is no harder for God to cope with them than with what we imagine to be our good deeds. I believe God is not just timeless fate, but that he waits upon and answers sincere prayer and responsible action.

Confidence

There is hardly one of us who has not known what it is to be betrayed. We used to find the figure of Judas an enigma, but now we know him only too well. The air we breathe is so infested with mistrust that it almost chokes us. But where we have managed to pierce through this layer of mistrust we have discovered a confidence scarce dreamed of hitherto. Where we do trust we have learnt to entrust our very lives to the hands of others. In face of all the many constructions to which our actions and our lives have been inevitably exposed we have learnt to trust without reserve. We know that hardly anything can be more reprehensible than the sowing and encouragement of mistrust, and that our duty is rather to do everything in our power to strengthen and foster confidence among men. Trust will always be one of the greatest, rarest and happiest blessings of social life, though it can only emerge on the dark background of a necessary mistrust. We have learnt never to trust a scoundrel an inch, but to give ourselves to the trustworthy without reserve.

The Sense of Quality

Unless we have the courage to fight for a revival of a wholesome reserve between man and man, all human values will be submerged in anarchy. The impudent contempt for such reserve is as much the mark of the rabble as interior uncertainty, as haggling and cringing for the favour of the insolent, as lowering oneself to the level of the rabble is the way to becoming no better than the rabble oneself. Where self-respect is abandoned, where the feeling for human quality and the power of reserve decay, chaos is at the door. Where impudence is tolerated for the sake of material comfort, self-respect is abandoned, the flood-gates are opened, and chaos bursts the dams we were pledged to defend. That is a crime against humanity. In other ages it may have been the duty of Christians to champion the equality of all men. Our duty to-day, however, is passionately to defend the sense of reserve between man and man. We shall be accused of acting for our own interests, of being anti-social. Such cheap jibes must be placidly accepted. They are the invariable protests of the rabble against decency and order. To be pliant and uncertain is to fail to realize what is at stake, and no doubt it goes a good way to justify those jibes. We are witnessing the levelling down of all ranks of society, but at the same time we are watching the birth of a new sense of nobility, which is binding together a circle of men from all the previous classes of society. Nobility springs from and thrives on self-sacrifice and courage and an unfailing sense of duty to oneself and society. It expects due deference to itself, but shows an equally natural deference to others, whether they be of higher or of lower degree. From start to finish it demands a recovery of a lost sense of quality and of a social order based upon quality. Quality is the bitterest enemy of conceit in all its forms. Socially it implies the cessation of all place-hunting, of the cult of the 'star'. It requires an open eye both upwards and downwards, especially in the choice of one's closest friends. Culturally it means a return from the newspaper and the radio to the book, from feverish activity to unhurried leisure, from dissipation to recollection, from sensationalism to reflection, from virtuosity to art, from snobbery to modesty, from extravagance to moderation. Quantities are competitive, qualities complementary.

Sympathy

We must never forget that most men only learn wisdom by personal experience. This explains, first, why so few people are capable of taking precautions in advance—they always think they will be able somehow or other to circumvent the danger. Secondly, it explains their insensibility to the sufferings of others. Sympathy grows in proportion to the fear of approaching disaster. There is a good deal of excuse on ethical grounds for this attitude. Nobody wants to meet fate head-on: inward calling and strength for action are only acquired in face of actual danger. Nobody is responsible for all the suffering and injustice in the world, and nobody wants to set himself up as the judge of the universe. Psychologically, our lack of imagination, sensitivity and mental agility is balanced by a steady composure, an unruffled power of concentration and an immense capacity for suffering. But from a Christian point of view, none of these mitigating circumstances can atone for the absence of the most important factor, that is, a real breadth of sympathy. Christ avoided suffering until his hour had come, but when it did come he seized it with both hands as a free man and mastered it. Christ, as the Scriptures tell us, bore all our human sufferings in his own body as if they were his own —a tremendous thought—and submitted to them freely. Of course, we are not Christs, we do not have to redeem the world by any action or suffering of our own. There is no need for us to lay upon ourselves such an intolerable burden. We are not lords, but instruments in the hand of the Lord of history. Our capacity to sympathize with others in their sufferings is strictly limited. We are not Christs, but if we want to be Christians we must show something of Christ's breadth of sympathy by acting responsibly, by grasping our 'hour', by facing danger like free men, by displaying a real sympathy which springs not from fear, but from the liberating and redeeming love of Christ for all who suffer. To look on without lifting a helping hand is most un-Christian. The Christian does not have to wait until he suffers himself; the sufferings of his brethren for whom Christ died are enough to awaken his active sympathy.

Of Suffering

It is infinitely easier to suffer in obedience to a human command than to accept suffering as free, responsible men. It is infinitely easier to suffer with others than to suffer alone. It is infinitely easier to suffer as public heroes than to suffer apart and in ignominy. It is infinitely easier to suffer physical death than to endure spiritual suffering. Christ suffered as a free man alone, apart and in ignominy, in body and in spirit, and since that day many Christians have suffered with him.

[24

Present and Future

We always used to think it was one of the elementary rights
of man that he should be able to plan his life in advance, both
private life and professional. That is a thing of the past. The
pressure of events is forcing us to give up 'being anxious for
the morrow'. But it makes all the difference in the world
whether we accept this willingly and in faith (which is what
the Sermon on the Mount means) or under compulsion. For
most people not to plan for the future means to live irresponsibly and frivolously, to live just for the moment, while some
few continue to dream of better times to come. But we cannot
take either of these courses. We are still left with only the
narrow way, a way often hardly to be found, of living every
day as if it were our last, yet in faith and responsibility living
as though a splendid future still lay before us. 'Houses and
fields and vineyards shall yet again be bought in this land',
cries Jeremiah just as the Holy City is about to be destroyed,
a striking contrast to his previous prophecies of woe. It is a
divine sign and pledge of better things to come, just when all
seems blackest. Thinking and acting for the sake of the coming
generation, but taking each day as it comes without fear and
anxiety—that is the spirit in which we are being forced to live
in practice. It is not easy to be brave and hold out, but it is
imperative.

Optimism

It is more prudent to be a pessimist. It is an insurance against
disappointment, and no one can say 'I told you so', which is
how the prudent condemns the optimist. The essence of
optimism is that it takes no account of the present, but it is a
source of inspiration, of vitality and hope where others have
resigned; it enables a man to hold his head high, to claim the
future for himself and not to abandon it to his enemy. Of
course there is a foolish, shifty kind of optimism which is
rightly condemned. But the optimism which is will for the

future should never be despised, even if it is proved wrong a hundred times. It is the health and vitality which a sick man should never impugn. Some men regard it as frivolous, and some Christians think it is irreligious to hope and prepare one-self for better things to come in this life. They believe in chaos, disorder and catastrophe. That, they think, is the meaning of present events, and in sheer resignation or pious escapism they surrender all responsibility for the preservation of life and for the generations yet unborn. To-morrow may be the day of judgement. If it is, we shall gladly give up working for a better future, but not before.

Insecurity and Death

During recent years we have come to know death at close quarters. We are sometimes startled at the placidity with which we hear of the death of one of our contemporaries. We cannot hate death as we used to, for we have discovered some good in it after all, and have almost come to terms with it. Fundamentally we feel that we really belong to death already, and that every new day is a miracle. It would hardly be true to say that we welcome death—although we all know that *accidie* which should be avoided like the plague—we are too curious for that, or to put it more seriously, we still hope to see some sense in the broken fragments of our life. Nor do we try and romanticize death, for life is too precious for that. Still less are we inclined to see in danger the meaning of life— we are not desperate enough for that, and we know too much about the joys life has to offer. And we know too much about life's anxieties also, and all the havoc wrought by prolonged insecurity. We still love life, but I do not think that death can take us by surprise now. After all we have been through during the war we hardly dare admit our hope that we shall not die a sudden and unexpected death for some trivial accident, but rather in dedication to some noble cause. It is not the external circumstances, but the spirit in which we face it, that makes death what it can be, a death freely and voluntarily accepted.

Are we still serviceable?

We have been the silent witnesses of evil deeds. Many storms have gone over our heads. We have learnt the art of deception and of equivocal speech. Experience has made us suspicious of others, and prevented us from being open and frank. Bitter conflicts have made us weary and even cynical. Are we still serviceable? It is not the genius that we shall need, not the cynic, not the misanthropist, not the adroit tactician, but honest, straightforward men. Will our spiritual reserves prove adequate and our candour with ourselves remorseless enough to enable us to find our way back again to simplicity and straightforwardness?

II

Letters to His Parents

April 14th 1943

My dear Parents,

I do want you to be quite sure that I am all right. I'm sorry this is the first time I have been allowed to write to you, but it was quite out of the question during the first ten days. To my surprise, the discomforts you usually associate with prison life, such as its physical hardships, don't seem to trouble me at all. I can even make a good breakfast each morning on dry bread, and sometimes I even get a few extra tit-bits. Still less am I worried about the hard prison bed, and I manage to get plenty of sleep between 8 p.m. and 6 a.m. Most surprising of all is that I have hardly felt the need for cigarettes since I came here. But I am quite sure that psychic factors have a good deal to do with it. It is such a violent upheaval, that it takes a lot to adjust the mind to it. Physical wants have to take a back seat for the time being, which is something I find a real enrichment of my experience. I am not so unused to solitude as some people would be, and it is quite as good as a turkish bath for the soul. The only thing that disturbs me is to think you might be worrying about me and not sleeping or eating properly. I really am sorry to cause you so much trouble, but it's not my fault—it's just my luck, that's all. What a great comfort Paul Gerhardt's hymns are! I am learning them off by heart. Then I have also got my Bible and some books out of the library here, and enough writing paper now . . .

It is now a fortnight since the 75th birthday. What a grand day that was! I can still hear the hymns we sang in the morning and evening, with all the voices and instruments. 'Praise to the Lord, the Almighty, the King of creation. . . . Shelters thee under his wings, yea, and gently sustaineth.' How true it is, and may it ever remain so! Spring is now on its way with a vengeance. You will have plenty to do in the garden. In the

[28

prison courtyard here there is a thrush which sings a beautiful little song every morning, and now he has started in the evening too. One is grateful for little things, and that also is a gain. Goodbye for now!

Easter Sunday
April 25th 1943

At last the tenth day has come round and I am allowed to write to you again. I do so want you to know that I am having a happy Easter in spite of everything. One of the great advantages of Good Friday and Easter Day is that they take us out of ourselves, and make us think of other things, of life and its meaning, and its sufferings and events. It gives us such a lot to hope for. Ever since yesterday it has been strangely quiet in the house. I heard many people wishing each other a happy Easter, and one can hardly begrudge them it, for it is a hard life, being a warder here.

First of all, let me thank you for all the things you brought for me. You can't imagine how thrilled I am when they tell me: 'Your mother and sister and brother have just been here with something for you.' The mere knowledge that you have been near me and have not forgotten me (of course I know there's really no danger of that!) is enough to keep me happy for the rest of the day. Thank you very, very much for everything!

Things are still going on all right, and I'm keeping well. Every day they let me out of doors for half an hour's exercise, and I am now allowed to smoke again. In fact, I often forget where I am! I can't complain about my treatment here. I read a good deal—newspapers, novels, and above all the Bible. I can't concentrate enough yet for serious work, but during Holy Week I at last managed to work through a part of the Passion story which has been worrying me for a long time— the High Priestly prayer of our Lord. And I have also studied some of the ethical sections of the Pauline Epistles, a useful piece of work. So there is still a lot to be thankful for.

It is surprising how quickly the day goes here. I can't believe

I have been here three weeks already. It is nice to go to bed at eight—supper is at four—and I enjoy my dreams. I never knew before what a source of pleasure that could be. I dream every day, and generally about something pleasant. I spend the time before I get to sleep saying over to myself the hymns I have learnt during the day, and when I wake up (about 6 a.m.) I like to read a few psalms and hymns, think about you all and remember that you are thinking about me.—The day is now over, and I hope you are feeling as contented as I am. I have read a lot of good things, and my thoughts and hopes have been pleasant too.

May 6th 1943

I have now had four weeks in prison, and whereas I had no difficulty from the outset in accepting my lot consciously, I am now getting used to it in a natural, unconscious sort of way. That is a relief, but it raises problems of its own, for I have no desire to get used to this sort of life, and it would not be right to, either. You would find it just the same.—You asked what life is like here. Well, just picture to yourself a cell. It does not need much imagination, in fact the less imagination you have the nearer the mark you will be. At Easter the *Deutsche Allgemeine Zeitung* brought out a reproduction from Dürer's Apocalypse, which I cut out and pinned up on the wall. Some of the primroses M. brought along are still here too. We are up fourteen hours, and I spend three of them walking up and down the cell—several miles a day, in addition to the half hour in the courtyard. The rest of the time I spend reading, learning things by heart and working. I particularly enjoyed reading Gotthelf again. What I like about him is his clear, wholesome, placid style. I am getting on all right and keeping well.

The wedding at S.'s will soon be here now. I shall not have a chance of writing again before the day. I have just read this in Jean Paul: 'The only joys which can stand the fires of adversity are the joys of home.' . . . I wish you a happy day from the bottom of my heart, and shall be with you in spirit.

[30

May your thoughts about me be confined to happy memories of the past and hopes for the future. It is when life goes hard that we particularly want to see the real joys of life unimpaired —and a wedding is certainly one of them.

I can't help thinking of that lovely song of Hugo Wolf which we sang a number of times recently:

> *Over night come joy and sorrow.*
> *Both are gone before to-morrow,*
> *Back to God to let him know*
> *How you've borne them here below.*

It all turns upon that 'how', far more than anything that happens to you from the outside. It allays all the anxieties about the future which so often torment us. Thank you for remembering me every day, and for all you are doing and putting up with for my sake. Best wishes to the family and friends. Tell R. she must not spoil her wedding by any regrets about me. She may rest assured that I am with her in spirit in all her happiness.

May 15th 1943

By the time this letter reaches you, all the preparations will be finished and the wedding itself will be over, including my own disappointment that I wasn't there myself. I am looking back with gratitude on all the blessing of the past and am rejoicing with them all. I wonder what the text of the sermon will be. The best I can think of is Romans 15.7, a text I have often used myself. . . . What marvellous summer weather they are having. I guess this morning's hymn was Paul Gerhardt's *Die güldne Sonne.*

Your letter has come at last. Many thanks. My parental home has become so much a part of myself that every time I hear from you I am overjoyed. If only we could at least see one another and have even a short chat, how lovely it would be, and what a relief!

People outside naturally find it difficult to imagine what

prison life must be like. In itself, that is, each single moment, life here is not very different from anywhere else, so far. I spend my time reading, meditating, writing, pacing up and down my cell—without rubbing myself sore on the walls like a polar bear! The important thing is to make the best use of one's possessions and capabilities—there are still plenty left—and to accept the limits of the situation, by which I mean not giving way to feelings of resentment and discontent. I have never realized so clearly what the Bible and Luther mean by spiritual trial. Quite suddenly, for no apparent reason, whether physical or psychological, the peace and placidity which have been a mainstay hitherto begin to waver, and the heart, in Jeremiah's expressive phrase, becomes that defiant and despondent thing one cannot fathom. It is like an invasion from outside, as though evil powers were trying to deprive one of life's dearest treasures. But it is a wholesome and necessary experience which helps one to a better understanding of human life. I am just trying my hand at an essay on 'The feeling of time' (*Zeitgefühl*), a topic of peculiar interest to one like myself who is held in custody for examination. Over the door of this cell one of my predecessors here has scribbled the words 'In 100 years it will all be over'. That was his way of trying to overcome the feeling that time spent here is a complete blank. There is much to be said on the subject, and I should like to talk it over with Papa. 'My time is in thy hand' (Psalm 31.16) —that is the Bible's answer. But there is also a question which the Bible asks, and which threatens to dominate the whole subject: 'Lord, how long?' (Psalm 13).

You really ought to read Gotthelf's *Berner Geist*, and if not the whole of it, at least the first part. It is quite unique, and will certainly interest you. I remember how old Schoene always had a special word of praise for Gotthelf, and I should like to suggest to the Diederich Press that they bring out a Gotthelf anthology. Stifter's background is mainly Christian. His woodland scenes often make me long to be back again in the quiet glades of Friedrichsbrunn. But he is not so forceful as Gotthelf, although he is wonderfully clear and simple, which gives me a great deal of pleasure. If only we could talk to one

[32

another about these things. For all my sympathy with the contemplative life, I am not a born Trappist! A temporary rule of silence may be a good thing, and Catholics tell us that the best expositions of Scripture come from the purely contemplative orders. I am reading the Bible straight through from cover to cover and have just got to the Book of Job, a firm favourite of mine. I am reading the Psalms daily, as I have done for years. I know them and love them more than any other book in the Bible. Whenever I read Psalms 3, 47, 70 and others, I always seem to hear them in the settings by Schütz. It was R. who first introduced me to his music, and I count it one of the greatest enrichments of my life.

I feel myself so much a part of you all that I know we live and bear everything in common, acting and thinking for one another even when we are separated.

III

A Wedding Sermon
from a Prison Cell

Ephesians 1.12: ' . . . to the end that we should be
unto the praise of his glory.'

IT IS wholly right and proper for a bride and bridegroom to
welcome their wedding day with a sense of triumph. All the
difficulties, obstacles, impediments, doubts and suspicions have
at last been—I shall not say, thrown to the winds, for that
would be to make too light of them—but honestly faced and
overcome. Both parties have now won the most important
battle of their lives. You have just said to one another 'I will',
and with those words you have declared your voluntary
assent and turned a critical point in your lives. You know full
well all the doubts and suspicions with which a lifelong part-
nership between two persons is faced. But you have defied
these doubts and suspicions with a cheerful confidence, and by
your free assent you have conquered a new land to live in.
Every wedding is an occasion of joy, joy that human beings
can do such great things, that they have been granted the
freedom and the power to take the rudder of their lives into
their own hands. The children of earth are rightly proud when
they are allowed a hand in shaping their own destinies. And
it is right that a bride and bridegroom should have this pride
on their wedding day. It would be wrong to speak too lightly
and irresponsibly about God's will and providence. To begin
with there can be no question that it is your own very human
wills which are at work here, which are celebrating their
triumph. The course you are embarking upon is one you
have chosen for yourselves. It is not in the first place something religious, but something quite secular. And so you alone
must bear the responsibility for what you are doing, it cannot
be taken from you. It is you, the bride and bridegroom, who

as a married couple must bear the whole responsibility for the success of your married life, with all the happiness it will bring. Unless you can boldly say to-day: 'This is *our* resolve, *our* love, *our* way', you are taking refuge in a false piety. 'Iron and steel may pass away, but *our* love shall abide for ever.' You hope to find in another that earthly bliss in which, to quote a mediæval song, the one is the comfort of the other both in body and in soul. Such a hope has its proper place in God's eyes as well as man's.

You have both been abundantly blessed in your lives up till now, and you have every reason to be thankful. The beauties and joys of life have almost overwhelmed you, success has always come your way, and you have been surrounded by the love of your friends. Your path has always been smoothed out before you. Amid all the changes and chances of life you have always been able to count on the support of both your families and your friends. Every one has been generous to you, and now you have found each other, and have at last been led to the goal of your desires. Such a life, as you know full well, can never be created or entered upon in our own power. It is given to some and denied to others. That is what we mean by divine providence. As you rejoice to-day that you have reached your goal, so you will be grateful that God's will and God's way have brought you hither. As you take full responsibility upon your own shoulders for what you are doing to-day, so with equal confidence you may place it all in the hands of God.

God has sealed your 'I will' with his own. He has crowned your assent with his. He has bestowed upon you this triumph and rejoicing and pride. He is thus making you the instruments of his will and purpose both for yourselves and for others. In his unfathomable condescension God veritably gives his Yea to yours. But in so doing he creates out of your love something that did not exist before—the holy estate of matrimony.

God is guiding your marriage. Marriage is more than your love for each other. It has a higher dignity and power. For it is God's holy ordinance, by means of which he wills to perpetuate the human race until the end of time. In your love you see your two selves as solitary figures in the world; in marriage you see yourselves as links in the chain of the generations, which God causes to come and go to his glory and calls into his kingdom. In your love you see only the heaven of your bliss, through marriage you are placed at a post of responsibility towards the world and to mankind. Your love is your own private possession; marriage is more than a private affair, it is an estate, an office. As the crown makes the king, and not just his determination to rule, so marriage and not just your love for each other makes you husband and wife in the sight of God and man. As you first gave the ring to one another and received it a second time from the hand of the parson, so love comes from you, but marriage from above, from God. As God is infinitely higher than man, so the sanctity, the privilege and the promise of marriage are higher than the sanctity, the privilege and promise of love. It is not your love which sustains the marriage, but from now on the marriage that sustains your love.

God makes your marriage indissoluble. 'Those whom God hath joined together, let not man put asunder.' God is joining you together: it is his act, not yours. Do not confound your love with God. God makes your marriage indissoluble, he protects it from every danger from within and without. What a blessed thing it is to know that no power on earth, no human frailty can dissolve what God holds together. Knowing that, we may say with all confidence, what God has joined together man *cannot* put asunder. No need now to be troubled with those anxious fears so inseparable from love. You can say to each other now without a shadow of doubt: 'We can never lose each other now. By the will of God we belong to each other till death us do part.'

God establishes an ordinance in which you can live together as man and wife. 'Wives, be in subjection to your husbands, as is fitting in the Lord. Husbands, love your wives, and be not bitter against them' (Colossians 3.18,19). With your love you are founding a home. That needs an ordinance, and this ordinance is so important that God establishes it himself, for without it life would be reduced to chaos. You may order

[36

your home as you like, save in one particular: the woman must
be subject to her husband, and the husband must love his wife.
In this way God gives to man and woman the glory peculiar
to each. It is the glory of the woman to serve the man and to
be a 'help meet' for him, as the creation story calls it. And it is
the glory of the man to love his wife with all his heart. He
'will leave his father and mother and cleave to his wife', he
will 'love her as his own flesh'. A woman who seeks to dominate her husband dishonours not only him but herself as well,
just as the man who does not love his wife as he should dishonours himself as well as her, and both dishonour the glory
of God which is meant to rest upon the estate of matrimony.
There is something wrong with a world in which the woman's
ambition is to be like a man, and in which the man regards
the woman as the toy of his lust for power and freedom. It is
a sign of social disintegration when the woman's service is
thought to be degrading, and when the man who is faithful to
his wife is looked upon as a weakling or a fool.

The place God has assigned for the woman is the husband's
home. Most people have forgotten nowadays what a home
can mean, though some of us have come to realize it as never
before. It is a kingdom of its own in the midst of the world,
a haven of refuge amid the turmoil of our age, nay more, a
sanctuary. It is not founded on the shifting sands of private
and public life, but has its peace in God. For it is God who
gave it its special meaning and dignity, its nature and privilege,
its destiny and worth. It is an ordinance God has established in
the world, the place where peace, quietness, joy, love, purity,
continence, respect, obedience, tradition, and, to crown them
all, happiness may dwell, whatever else may pass away in the
the world. It is the woman's calling and her joy to build up
this world within the world for her husband, and to make it
the scene of her activity. How happy she is when she realizes
what a noble and rich destiny and task is hers. Not novelty,
but permanence, not change, but constancy, not noisiness, but
peace, not words, but deeds, not peremptoriness, but persuasion,
and all these things inspired and sustained by her love for her
husband—such is the woman's kingdom. In the Book of

37]

Proverbs we read: 'The heart of her husband trusteth in her. And he shall have no lack of gain. She doeth him good and not evil all the days of her life. She seeketh wool and flax, and worketh willingly with her hands. She riseth also while it is yet night. And giveth meat to her household. And their task is to their maidens. . . . She spreadeth out her hand to the poor; yea, she reacheth forth her hands to the needy. . . . Strength and dignity are her clothing; And she laugheth at the time to come. . . . Her children rise up, and call her blessed; her husband also, and he praiseth her, saying, Many daughters have done virtuously, But thou excellest them all.' Again and again the Bible praises, as the supreme happiness which earth affords, the fortune of a man who finds a true, or as the Bible itself calls her, a 'virtuous' or 'wise' woman. 'Her price is far above rubies.' 'A virtuous woman is a crown to her husband.' But the Bible can speak just as frankly of the woe which the perverse or 'foolish' woman can bring upon her husband and her home.

The Bible goes on to call the man the head of the woman, adding also 'even as Christ is the Head of the Church'. Something of the divine splendour is here reflected in our earthly relationships, and this reflection is something we should recognize and honour. The dignity ascribed to the man lies not in any quality of his own, but in the office conferred upon him by his marriage. The woman should see her husband arrayed in this dignity. But for him it is his supreme responsibility. As the head, it is he who is responsible for his wife, for their marriage, and for their home. On him falls the care and protection of the family. He represents it to the outside world, he is its mainstay and comfort; he is the master of the house, who exhorts, helps, comforts, and stands as their priest before God. It is good thing, for it is a divine ordinance when the woman honours the man for his office's sake, and when the man properly discharges the duties of his office. The man and woman who acknowledge and observe the ordinance of God are 'wise', but those who think they can replace it by another of their own devising are 'foolish'.

God has laid upon marriage both a blessing and a burden.

The blessing is the promise of children. God allows man to co-operate with him in the work of creation and preservation. But it is always God himself who blesses marriage with children. 'Children are a gift that cometh of the Lord' (Psalm 127), and they should be acknowledged as such. It is from God that parents receive their children, and it is to him that they should lead them. Hence parents exercise an authority over their children which is derived from God. Luther says that God invests parents with a chain of gold, and Scripture annexes to the fifth commandment the promise of long life on earth. But since men live on earth, God has given them a lasting reminder that this earth stands under the curse of sin and is not itself the ultimate reality. Over the destiny of woman and of man lies the dark shadow of the wrath of God. The woman must bear her children in pain, and in providing for his family the man must reap many thorns and thistles and labour in the sweat of his brow. This burden should drive both man and wife to call on God and should remind them of their eternal destiny in his kingdom. Earthly society is but the beginning of that eternal society, the earthly home the image of the heavenly, the earthly family the symbol of the Fatherhood of God over men, who are all his children.

God intends you to found your marriage on Christ. 'Wherefore receive ye one another, even as Christ also received you, to the glory of God.' In a word, live together in the forgiveness of your sins, for without it no human fellowship, least of all a marriage, can survive. Don't insist on your rights, don't blame each other, don't judge or condemn each other, don't find fault with each other, but take one another as you are, and forgive each other every day from the bottom of your hearts.

From the first day of your marriage until the last your rule must be: 'Receive one another . . . to the praise of God.'

Such is the word of God for your marriage. Thank him for it, thank him for bringing you thus far. Ask him to establish your marriage, to confirm and hallow it and preserve it to the end. With this your marriage will be 'to the praise of his glory'. Amen.

IV

Letters to His Parents

. . . Thank you very much for your letters. They are always too short for *me*, but of course I understand! It is as though the prison gates were opened for a moment, and I could share a little of your life outside. Joy is something we can do with very badly here; it's such a serious place, no one ever laughs. It seems to get even the warders down.

To-day is Ascension Day, and a day of great joy for all who can believe that Christ rules the world and our lives. My thoughts go out to all of you, to the Church and its services, from which I have been cut off so long. Nor do I forget those unknown people in this house who are bearing their fate in silence. I find such thoughts as these a good antidote against thinking too much of my own hardships. It would be wrong of me and most ungrateful to give way to that temptation.

I have just written a bit more of my essay on *Zeitgefühl*. I enjoy writing it very much. When I write from personal experience, I find it flows easily from the pen, and it helps me to get it all off my chest. Thank you for sending Kant's *Anthropology*, Papa. I hadn't read it before, but I've got all through it now. Much of it was interesting, but I think his psychology is too rationalistic and rococo, and there are many phenomena which it simply ignores. Can you send me something on the subject of memory, its various forms and functions? It's a topic one is naturally very interested in here. I enjoyed Kant's opinion about smoking as a means of solitary amusement.

I am awfully glad to hear you are reading Gotthelf. You will certainly like his *Wanderungen* just as much. For serious reading I have read here Uhlhorn's *Geschichte der christlichen Liebestätigkeit* with much enjoyment. It reminded me of the Church History we learnt in Holl's seminar.

I read some Stifter almost every day. The intimate life of his characters—it is so old-fashioned of him only to depict sympathetic characters—does me a lot of good in this atmosphere here, and guides one's thoughts to the things that really matter in life. In every way life in prison makes one return to the simplest things in life. That explains for instance why I have found it impossible to get along with Rilke. Though I wonder whether one's understanding is not affected by the restrictions under which one has to live. . . .

Whitsunday
June 14th 1943

Well, Whitsun is here, and we are still separated from one another. Yet it is in quite a special way a feast of fellowship. When I heard the church bells ringing this morning, I felt how I should have loved to go to church, but instead I followed St. John's example on the isle of Patmos, and held a nice little service of my own. I hardly felt lonely at all, for I was quite sure you were with me, and so were all the congregations with whom I have kept Whitsun in previous years. Every hour or so since yesterday morning I have been repeating to myself the words: 'Thou art a Spirit of joy', and 'Grant us strength and power'. These words are a great comfort—from Paul Gerhardt's Whitsun hymn, which I love so much, and then the words: 'If thou faint in the day of adversity, thy strength is small', from Proverbs 24; and 'God gave us not a spirit of fearfulness, but of power and love and discipline', from II Timothy 1. The strange story of the first Whitsunday, with its miraculous gift of tongues, has once more provided a good deal of food for thought. At the tower of Babel all the tongues were confounded, and as a result men could no longer understand one another as they all spoke different languages. This confusion is now brought to an end by the language of God, which is universally intelligible and the only means of mutual understanding among men. And the Church is the place where that miracle happens.—Truly, these are noble and inspiring thoughts. All his life Leibniz toyed with the idea of

41]

a universal script consisting not of words but of self-evident signs in which he hoped every conceivable idea might be expressed. In this way he hoped that all the divisions in the world of his day might be healed. It is a sort of philosophical reflex of the Pentecost story.—Once again, all is quiet here, except for the tramp of the prisoners pacing up and down in their cells. And how comfortless and un-Whitsun-like some of their thoughts must be! If I were prison chaplain here I should spend the whole time from morn to night on days like this visiting the prisoners in their cells. What a lot would happen then! . . .

You are all waiting, like me, and I must admit I had a sort of unconscious feeling that I should be out of here by Whitsun, although on the conscious level I am always telling myself not to pin my hopes on any definite date. To-morrow I shall have been here ten weeks. As mere laymen little did we dream that 'temporary confinement' would be so long as this! It is a great mistake to be so ignorant of legal affairs as I am. It brings home to one what a different atmosphere the lawyer must live in compared with the theologian. But that is another salutary lesson, and there is a proper place for everything. All we can do is to trust they are making every effort to get things cleared up as quickly as possible. So we must try hard to be patient, and not get bitter. Fritz Reuter puts it very well: 'No one's life flows on such an even course that it does not sometimes come up against a dam and whirl round and round, or somebody throws a stone into the clear water. Something happens to everyone—and he must take care that the water stays clear and that heaven and earth are reflected in it'—when you've said that you have really said everything.

My essay on *Zeitgefühl* is practically finished. I am going to let it simmer for a while and see what it looks like later.

It is Whitmonday, and I was just sitting down to a dinner of turnips and potatoes when the parcel you sent me by Ruth as a present for Whitsun arrived. Such things give me greater joy than I can say. Although I am utterly convinced that nothing can break the bonds between us, I seem to need some outward token or sign to reassure me. In this way

[42

material things become vehicles of spiritual realities. I suppose it's rather like the need felt in all religions for sacraments.

June 24th 1943

What a blessing it is in such times as this to belong to a large and closely-knit family where each trusts the other and stands by him. I often used to think when pastors were sent to prison that it was easier for those who were unmarried. But I had no idea then what the love of wife and family could mean in the coldness of prison life, and how in just such times of separation the feeling of belonging together through thick and thin is actually intensified. . . .

Some letters have just arrived, for which I thank you very much. From what you say about the strawberries and raspberries, of school holidays and plans for travel, I begin to feel summer has really come. One hardly notices here the passing of the seasons. I am glad the weather is so seasonable. Just recently I discovered a tomtit's nest in the courtyard with ten young. I enjoyed going to look at it everyday until someone went and destroyed the lot. To think that anyone could be so cruel! Some of the tomtits were lying dead on the ground, poor things. There is also a small ant-hill, and some bees in the lime trees. These things add a good deal of enjoyment to my walks in the courtyard. I often think of the story of Peter Bamm who lived on a beautiful island where he met all sorts of people, good and bad. One night, however, he had a nightmare and dreamt that the day might come when the whole lot would be obliterated by a bomb, but all he could think of was what a pity it would be for the butterflies! Prison life brings home to a man how nature carries on its quiet, care-free life quite unconcerned, and makes one feel almost sentimental towards animal and plant life—except for flies; I can't work up any sentiment about them! The prisoner finds compensation for the lack of warmth and cordiality in his surroundings in an exaggerated sentimentality. When this happens to me I find it is a good thing to call myself to order with a cold shower of sobriety and humour. If I didn't do this I should be completely knocked off my balance. I believe it is just here that Christianity, rightly understood, can help immensely.

All this will be no news to you, Papa, with your long experience of prisoners. I am not yet sure what exactly prison psychosis, as they call it, is, though I have a pretty shrewd idea.

July 3rd 1943

About six o'clock on a Sunday evening the bells of the prison chapel start ringing, and that is the best moment to write home. What an extraordinary power church bells have over us human beings, and how deeply they affect us. So many associations have gathered around them. All our discontents, ingratitude and self-seeking vanish away, and in a moment only our pleasant memories remain hovering around us like benign spirits. First I recall those quiet summer evenings in Friedrichsbrunn, then all the different parishes I have worked in, and then all our family occasions, weddings, christenings and confirmations—to-morrow my godchild will be confirmed. Innumerable memories come crowding in upon me, but only those which inspire peace, gratitude and confidence. If only I could be a greater help to others! During the past week I have done a good deal of quiet work and have read some good books, as well as some letters from you. And now to-day there is your magnificent parcel. What a pity you have had to have the windows of the air raid shelter walled in!

I have now been three months in prison. I remember Schlatter once saying in his Ethics lectures that it was one of the duties of a Christian citizen to take it patiently when he was arrested for investigation. It didn't mean a thing to me at the time, but just lately I have been thinking about it quite a lot. So let us keep on waiting quietly and patiently as long as it will be required of us, and as we have been doing up to now.

I often dream that I have been released and am back home again with you. . . . The day lilies are simply marvellous. Their cups open slowly in the morning and bloom only for a day,

[44

and next morning there are fresh ones to take their place. The day after to-morrow they will all be over.

Sunday
July 27th 1943

To think you came here yesterday in all that heat to bring me the parcel! I hope it hasn't exhausted you too much. Many thanks for coming and for all the things you brought for me. The summer produce is particularly welcome, of course. Fancy the tomatoes being ripe already! I am feeling the warmth for the first time just now. But it is not too unpleasant in the cell, especially as I keep pretty still most of the time. The only trouble is that I long more and more for fresh air. If only I could spend an evening in the garden again! It's nice to have the half-hour's exercise every day, but it is not enough. I seem to have a permanent cold, and I don't suppose I shall be able to shake it off until I get out into the open air again. The flowers here are a great blessing; they bring some colour and life into this dreary cell.

In my reading I am now concentrating wholly on the nineteenth century. During recent months I have read Gotthelf, Stifter, Immermann, Fontane and Keller with sheer admiration. There couldn't have been much wrong with an age which could write such simple and lucid German. They treat the most delicate matters without the slightest trace of flippancy, and can express their convictions without pathos—no exaggerated simplifying or complicating either in language or subject matter; in short, I find them extremely attractive. They must have taken great pains over their style, which means they must have had plenty of opportunity for quiet. By the way the last Reuters were as fascinating as ever; their equipoise extends even to the language, and fills me with joy and amazement. An author's style is often by itself enough to attract or repel.

Each time I hope this will be my last letter from prison. Surely every day makes my release more probable. I am gradually beginning to feel I have had enough of it. If only we could have a few of these lovely summer days together!

August 3rd 1943

I am glad I can write to you oftener now, and very grateful too. For I fear you must often be worrying about me, not only on account of the heat in my cell just under the roof, but also because I asked you to procure for me the services of a lawyer. That wonderful parcel of yours has just arrived, with tomatoes, apples, bottled fruit, thermos flask, etc., and that fantastic cooling salt.—I never knew such a thing existed. What a lot of trouble you have taken for me again. Please don't worry. I have often had to put up with worse heat in Italy, Africa, Spain, Mexico, and almost the worst of all was in New York in July 1939, so I have a pretty shrewd idea how to keep myself as comfortable as possible in it. I eat and drink very little and sit quietly at my desk, and in this way manage to work without hindrance. From time to time I refresh both body and soul with your wonderful things. I don't want to put in for a transfer to another floor, as it would not be fair on the other man who would have to be moved up here, and I don't suppose he would have any tomatoes, etc. Besides, it does not make much difference whether the temperature in the cell is 93 or only 86. I am sorry Hans[1] finds the heat so trying. It is wonderful what you can put up with when you know you've got to, but quite different when you think there is a chance of relief round the corner.

I hope you have not been worrying since I asked you to procure me a lawyer. You must wait for things to take their course, like me. Don't imagine I am restless or depressed. Of course the delay was a disappointment for me, as I suppose it was for you too. But somehow it's a consolation to know that my case will soon be cleared up after we have been on tenterhooks for so long. Every day I am hoping for more details about the procedure.

Once again I have been reading a lot of good things. *Jürg Jenatsch* refreshed a youthful memory and gave me a good deal of pleasure and interest. As regards history, I found the work

---

[1] Hans von Dohnanyi, in the Lehrterstrasse prison at the same time.

[46

about the Venetians very instructive and arresting. Would you please send me some Fontane: *Frau Jenny Treibel, Irrungen, Wirrungen* and *Stechlin*? I am bound to reap the benefit of this concentrated reading of the past few months, it will help me a great deal in the work I am planning. One often learns more about ethics from such books as these than from the text-books. I enjoyed Reuter's *Kein Hüsung* as much as you did, Mama. Surely I must have finished the Reuters by now—or is there still something very special in store for me?

The other day I read this pretty verse in *Der Grüne Heinrich*:

> *The waves of the sea may roar*
> *And do their worst against me,*
> *I hear your song as of yore,*
> *Not a single note can escape me.*

August 7th 1943

How are you getting on with the A.R.P.? After all that has been in the papers these last few days one cannot help thinking out the whole matter afresh. Do you remember we were rather doubtful about the supports in the cellar, and talked about having the central beam reinforced? I wonder if you have thought any more about it, and whether it would be possible to get someone to help you with the work. I daresay it would be difficult now. How I should love to come and help you myself. Let me know all about it anyhow. I am interested in every detail.

I don't think I told you that every day, when I get tired of reading and writing, I amuse myself with a chess problem. If you come across some good little work on the subject I should be grateful, but don't put yourself out about it. I shall manage. . . .

August 17th 1943

. . . Above all, please don't worry over me unduly. I'm keeping my end up, and am quite content at heart. What a good thing it is to know from previous experience that there is no need for air raids to alarm us unduly! I am very glad the law courts are to stay in Berlin. In the meantime we've all got better things to do than to be thinking all the time about possible air raids. Prison life seems to give one a certain detachment from the alarums and excitements of the day. . . .

For the past fortnight everything has been so uncertain that I have not felt like any serious work. But now I am going to try and get down to some more writing. Some weeks ago I tried to sketch out a play, but meanwhile I have discovered that the theme does not really lend itself to dramatic treatment, so I shall try and rewrite it as a story. It is about the life of a family. As you would expect, there is a good deal of autobiography mixed up in it.

The death of the three young pastors is a great personal loss to me. I should be grateful if their relatives could be told that I cannot write to them at present, otherwise they might not understand. These three were my most promising pupils. It is a sad blow, both for me personally, and for the Church. More than thirty of my pupils must have fallen by now, and nearly all of them were among my best. . . .

August 24th 1943

What a lively time you had last night. I was much relieved to hear from the head warder that you were all right. My cell is high up, and the window is kept wide open during the alarm, so I get a grandstand view of the awful fireworks on the south side of the city. It's not that I feel personally discontented with my lot, but I can't help feeling during these raids how utterly absurd it is to be kept waiting here doing nothing. The *Brüdergemeinde* text for this morning was most appropriate: 'I will give peace in the land, and ye shall lie down, and none shall make you afraid' (Leviticus 26.6).

On Sunday night I stupidly got a touch of gastric trouble. Yesterday I had a temperature, but to-day it's back to normal. I have only just got up to write this letter, and I intend to go straight back to bed again as a precaution. I don't want to be

[48

ill here if I can help it. As there are no special arrangements for sick diet, I was very pleased with your rusks and a packet of biscuits I kept by me for such emergencies. A medical orderly also gave me some of his white bread, so I am able to get along pretty well. I ought to have something of the kind here in case of emergencies, and perhaps also a small packet of semolina or oat flakes, which I could have cooked for me. But by the time you get this letter, the matter will be a thing of the past. . . .

August 31st 1943

For the last day or two I have been back again to normal and have got quite a lot of writing done. When I find myself back in the cell after a few hours of complete absorption in my work it takes me a moment or two to get my bearings again. It still seems incredible that I am here. However much I get used to the external conditions of prison life, it doesn't seem natural.

It is quite interesting to watch this gradual process of self-adaptation. I was given a knife and fork to eat with a week ago—a new concession—and they seemed almost unnecessary, it had become so natural to spread bread, etc., with a spoon. But there are other things which are so irrational, e.g. the actual state of being in prison, that it is impossible to get used to them, or at least very hard. The only thing to do is to accept it quite consciously. Surely there must be some books on the psychology of prison life?

Delbrück's *History of the World* makes good reading, though it seems to be more of a history of Germany. I have finished *Die Mikrobenjäger*, and enjoyed it very much. Otherwise I have been reading some more Storm, though I can't say I was very much impressed by it on the whole. I do hope you're going to bring me some more Fontane or Stifter. . . .

September 5th 1943

There is no need to compare notes about the night before last. The view from the window was unforgettable—the livid sky, etc. What a relief when the warder told me next morning that you were safe. It is remarkable how we think at such times about those we should not like to live without, and forget all about ourselves. It makes one realize how closely our lives are bound up with other people's, and in fact how our centre is outside of ourselves and how little we are individuals. To say 'as though it were a part of me'[1] is perfectly true, as I have often found after hearing that one of my colleagues or pupils has fallen. I think it is a literal fact of nature that human life extends far beyond our physical existence. Probably a mother feels this more than anybody. There are however two passages in the Bible which to my mind sum it all up better than anything else. One is from Jeremiah 45: 'Behold, that which I have built will I break down, and that which I have planted I will pluck up. . . . And seekest thou great things for thyself? Seek them not: . . . . but thy life will I give unto thee for a prey'; and the other from Psalm 60: 'Thou hast moved the land and divided it; heal the sores thereof for it shaketh.' . . .

I wish you would let me know whether you have had the anti-shrapnel trench dug, and whether it is not possible to make an exit from the cellar to the trench. Captain M. has had one made for himself.

I am still getting on all right. I have been moved two floors lower on account of the raids, and I now have a direct view on to the Church towers from my window, which is very nice. This last week or so I have been able to write quite well again. The only thing I miss is exercise in the open air, which I still depend upon a great deal for any really worthwhile work. But it won't be long now, and that's the main thing.

September 13th 1943

Last time I said I should like to have more letters, and now a whole sheaf has arrived to-day. You can imagine how glad

[1] *'als wär's ein Stück von mir'* from the soldier's song, *Ich hatt' einen Kameraden.* (Translator.)

I am. A day when the post comes is a red letter day which breaks the drab monotony of prison life. I have also been granted permission to speak to visitors, so things are now looking up. After the wretched delay in the delivery of mail this last week or two I have felt very grateful for that. I was glad you seemed a little better when you came. What depresses me more than any other aspect of the case is that you were not able to get away for the holiday you so badly needed. You must get away before winter—and how wonderful it would be if I could come too! . . .

It's a queer feeling to be so utterly dependent on the help of others, but at least it teaches one to be grateful, a lesson I hope I shall never forget. In normal life we hardly realize how much more we receive than we give, and life cannot be rich without such gratitude. It is so easy to overestimate the importance of our own achievements compared with what we owe to the help of others.

The turbulent events in the world outside during the last few days make me feel how much I should like to be somewhere where I could be useful. But for the time being my job is to stay in prison, and what I can do here makes its contribution in the unseen world, though that hardly comes under the category of active service. I often think of Schubert's *Münnich* and his crusade.

For the rest I am reading and writing for all I am worth, and am glad to say I've never had a moment's boredom, although I have been here more than five months now. My time is always fully occupied, but in the background there is always a gnawing sense of waiting for something to happen.

A few weeks ago I asked you to get me some new books: N. Hartmann's *Systematische Philosophie*, and *Das Zeitalter des Marius und Sulla*, published by Diederichs. Now I should also like *Die Deutsche Musik* by R. Benz. I would not like to miss these things, and should be glad to get them read while I am still here. K. F. wrote about a book on physics written for the layman, and said he would send it to me. I have practically finished everything worth reading here. Perhaps I shall have another go at Jean Paul's *Siebenkäs* or *Flegeljahren*. I have them here in my room. I don't suppose I should ever tackle them again, and there are well-read people who think a lot of them. But despite several attempts I have always found him long-winded and too full of mannerisms. But as we are in the middle of September, I hope these wishes will already be out of date before they are fulfilled.

September 25th 1943

I should like it much better if one were told in advance how long a business like this was likely to last. Even in my work here there is much that I could have done differently and more profitably. The way we are made, every day and every week are precious. Paradoxical though it may sound, I was really glad yesterday when first the permission for a lawyer and then the warrant for my arrest came. So it seems that the apparently purposeless waiting will soon be at an end. All the same, being in custody so long has been an experience I shall never forget. . . . For the rest, I am getting some writing done, and am noticing that I also enjoy non-theological authors. For the first time in my life I have discovered how difficult the German language can be, and how easily it can be spoilt. . . .

Reading this letter through, I notice it sounds rather disgruntled. I did not mean it to be so. Much as I long to be out of here, I don't believe a single day has been wasted. What will come out of my time here it is too early to say. But something is bound to come out of it. . . .

October 4th 1943

What delightful autumn weather we are having! If only you were at Friedrichsbrunn, and I with you, and Hans and his family too! But there must be thousands who cannot have what they want. I can't agree with Diogenes that the *summum bonum* is the absence of desire, or that the best place to live in is a tub. Why should we pretend that all our geese are swans?

[52

All the same I do believe it is good for us not to have everything we want, especially when we are young, though it would be wrong to give up wishing for anything, for then we should grow apathetic. But there is no danger of that happening to me at the moment.

A letter from C. has just arrived. It is astonishing how his mind keeps preying on the subject. What effect it must have on a fourteen year old lad to have to write to his father and godfather in prison for months on end! He cannot have many illusions left about the world. No doubt all this means the end of his childhood. Please thank him for his letter—I am very much looking forward to seeing him again.

I am glad you were able to get hold of Hartmann's *Systematische Philosophie*. I am getting down to it properly, and it will keep me going for several weeks, if the interruption I hope for does not occur in the meantime. . . .

October 13th 1943

I have in front of me the gay bunch of dahlias you brought me yesterday. It is a reminder of the lovely hour I was allowed to have with you, and it also reminds me of the garden and of the loveliness of the world in general. One of Storm's verses I came across the other day seems to express my mood, and keeps going through my head like a tune one cannot get rid of:

> *And though the world outside be mad,*
> *Christian or unchristian,*
> *Yet the world, the beautiful world*
> *Is utterly indestructible.*[1]

All I need to bring that home to me is a few autumn flowers, the view from my cell window, and half an hour's exercise in

[1] *Und geht es draussen noch so toll,*
unchristlich oder christlich,
ist doch die Welt, die schöne Welt
so gänzlich unverwüstlich.

the courtyard, where the chestnuts and limes are looking lovely. But in the last resort, the world, for me at any rate, consists of those few we would like to see, and whose company we long to share. . . . And if I could also hear a good sermon on Sundays—I often hear fragments of the chorales carried up here on the breeze—it would be better still.

Once again I have been doing a good deal of writing. The day seems much too short for all the work I want to get through—strangely enough I have often had the feeling here that there was 'no time' here for work and for less important matters! After breakfast every morning (about 7 o'clock) I read some theology, then I write until midday; in the afternoon I read, and then comes a chapter out of Delbrück's *History of the World*, and some English grammar—of which I still have a lot to learn, and finally, as the mood takes me, I read or write again. . . .

October 31st 1943

. . . To-day is Reformation Day, a feast which in our times can give one plenty to think about. One wonders how it was Luther's action led to consequences which were the exact opposite of what he intended, and which overshadowed the last years of his life and work, so that he doubted the value of everything he had achieved. He desired a real unity both for the Church and for Western Christendom, but the consequence was the ruin of both. He sought the 'Freedom of the Christian Man', and the consequence was apathy and barbarism. He hoped to see the establishment of a genuine social order free from clerical privilege, and the outcome was the Peasants' Revolt, and soon afterwards the gradual dissolution of all real cohesion and order in society. I remember from my student days a debate between Holl and Harnack as to whether in any movement it was the primary or the secondary motives which finally prevailed. At the time I thought Holl was right in maintaining that it was the former. To-day I am sure he was wrong. Kierkegaard said more than a century ago that if Luther were alive then he would have said the exact opposite of what he said

[54

in the sixteenth century. I believe he was right—*cum grano salis*.

Now a further request. Would you please order for me: *Lesebuch der Erzähler*, by Wolf-Dietrich Rasch (published by Kiepenheuer, 1943), *Die Ballade* by Wilhelm von Scholz (published by Theodor Knauer, 1943), *Briefe der Liebe aus 8 Jahrhunderten* by Friedrich Reck-Malleszewen (published by Keil, 1943)? Perhaps the editions are not large, and therefore they must be ordered at once.

A short time ago my rheumatism was so bad that I could not get up from my chair without help or lift my hands to feed myself. But they at once gave me electrical treatment in the sick ward, and it is much better now, though I have not been completely free of it since May. Is there anything I could do about it later? . . .

November 9th 1943

I was very surprised and pleased with the Stifter Anthology. As it consists mainly of extracts from his letters it was almost new to me. My overriding interest for the last ten days has been the *Witiko*, which, after my giving you so much trouble to hunt for it, was discovered in the library here, the last place I should have expected to find it. Most people to-day would find its 1,000 pages—which cannot be skipped, but have to be read quietly—altogether beyond them, and so I am uncertain whether to recommend it to you or not. But for me it is one of the most beautiful books I know. The purity of his style and his character-drawing gives one a rare and unique feeling of bliss. I really should have started at the age of fourteen with this book instead of the *Kampf um Rom*, and then have grown up with it. It is definitely *sui generis*. I should love to possess it, but it would hardly be possible to get hold of it. The only historical romances which have made any comparable impression on me hitherto are *Don Quixote* and Gotthelf's *Berner Geist*. I have had another shot at Jean Paul, but still can't make anything of him. I can't get away from the feeling that he is flippant and too full of mannerisms. He must have been just as odious as a man too.—It is lovely to go like this on voyages of literary discovery, and it is amazing what surprises one comes across after so many years of reading. Perhaps you have further suggestions to make?

A few days ago I had a letter from R., for which I thank him very much. It made my mouth water to read the pro-gramme of the Furtwängler concert he was at. I hope I shan't forget what still remains of my technique while I am here. I often get downright hungry for a trio, a quartet, or an even-ing's sing-song. My ear longs for a change from the voices in this building. More than seven months here is really quite enough. But of course that is only to be expected, and there's no need to mention it to you. The wonderful thing however is that I am getting on all right here, that I have many little pleasures, and manage to keep cheerful all the time. So I've got a lot to be thankful for every day. . . .

November 17th 1943

To-day is Repentance Day, and as I write this letter the S.'s are all listening to the B Minor Mass. For years now I have associated it with this particular day like the St. Matthew Passion with Good Friday. I have a vivid recollection of the evening I first heard it. I was eighteen, and had just come from Harnack's seminar. He had been discussing my first seminar essay very kindly, and said he hoped that some day I should specialize in Church History. I was full of this when I entered the Philharmonic Hall, where the great *Kyrie Eleison* was just beginning. In a moment it put everything else out of my mind: it was an indescribable impression. To-day I am going through the whole work bit by bit in my mind, and am glad the S.'s can hear it, my favourite work of Bach.

It is nearly evening now, and all quiet in the house. So I can pursue my thoughts undisturbed. In the course of the day I keep on discovering how noisy men can be at their work. No doubt they were born like it. A *fortissimo* just outside my cell is hardly the right background for serious study.

I have been re-reading Goethe's *Reinecke Fuchs* this last week with great enjoyment. Perhaps it would amuse you too.

[56

Advent Sunday
November 28th 1943

I have no notion how my letters are reaching you at the present moment. I don't even know whether you are getting them at all. But as it's Advent Sunday, I do just want to write to you this afternoon. Altdorfer's Nativity is very topical this year, with its picture of the Holy Family and the crib beneath a ruined house—how did he come to defy tradition in this way four hundred years ago? Was his meaning that Christmas could and should be kept even under such conditions as these? Anyhow, that is his message for us. I love to think of you sitting down with the children and keeping Advent as you used to years ago with us. The only difference is that we enter into it more intensely to-day, since we know not how much longer it is likely to last.

It still makes me shudder when I think what an awful night you had, and one really dreadful moment, without either of us with you. I can't see why I should be shut up in times like these with nothing to do. I do hope it will soon be over now, and that there won't be much more delay. All the same, don't worry about me. We shall come out of it all much strengthened.

The long-awaited attack on near-by Borsig has come at last, as you know already. One can't help hoping, though it's not a very Christian hope, that our district will now be spared for some time. It wasn't exactly pleasant, and when I am released, I shall offer a few suggestions for the improvement of the organization here during incidents of this kind. By a miracle not a pane of glass was broken in my windows, whereas nearly all the others are gone completely. It makes it terribly cold for the other men. Owing to the partial destruction of the prison wall all exercise has been temporarily suspended. If only we could hear from one another after an attack!

These last few days I have been enjoying H. W. Riehl's *Geschichten aus alten Zeiten*. Perhaps you remember the book from earlier times. To-day it is well-nigh forgotten, though it's still a good book and enjoyable to read. It would also be suitable for reading aloud to the children. I seem to remember we used to have some of his works at home, but they must have been given away for some bazaar or other.

It would be nice if you could bring me the book on superstition. They have started consulting the cards here about the chances of a raid during the coming night. It is interesting how superstition thrives in times like these, and how many are ready to listen, at least with half an ear.

December 17th 1943

I am writing my Christmas letter already so as to be on the safe side. If, contrary to all expectation, I should still be here at Christmas, the past eight and a half months have taught me that it is the unexpected that happens, and that the inevitable must be accepted with a *sacrificium intellectus*, though the *sacrificium* is never quite complete, and the *intellectus* still goes its own sweet way.

I am not going to let this lonely Christmas get me down. It will always take its place among the other unusual Christmasses of my life, in Spain, Africa, America and England. In years to come I shall not look back on this Christmas with shame, but with a certain pride. That is the only thing no one can take away from me.

Of course you can't help thinking of my being in prison over Christmas, and it is bound to throw a shadow over the few hours of happiness which still await you in these times. All I can do to help is to assure you that I know you will keep it in the same spirit as I do, for we are agreed on how Christmas ought to be kept. How could it be otherwise when my attitude to Christmas is a heritage I owe to you? I need not tell you how much I long to be released and to see you all again. But for years you have given us such lovely Christmasses, that our grateful memories are strong enough to cast their rays over a darker one. In times like these we learn as never before what it means to possess a past and a spiritual heritage untrammelled by the changes and chances of the present. A spiritual heritage reaching back for centuries is a wonderful support and comfort

[58

in face of all temporary stresses and strains. I believe that the man who is aware of such reserves of power need not be ashamed of the tender feelings evoked by the memory of a rich and noble past, for such feelings belong in my opinion to the better and nobler part of mankind. They will not overwhelm those who hold fast to values of which no man can deprive them.

For a Christian there is nothing peculiarly difficult about Christmas in a prison cell. I daresay it will have more meaning and will be observed with greater sincerity here in this prison than in places where all that survives of the feast is its name. That misery, suffering, poverty, loneliness, helplessness and guilt look very different to the eyes of God from what they do to man, that God should come down to the very place which men usually abhor, that Christ was born in a stable because there was no room for him in the inn—these are things which a prisoner can understand better than anyone else. For him the Christmas story is glad tidings in a very real sense. And that faith gives him a part in the communion of saints, a fellowship transcending the bounds of time and space and reducing the months of confinement here to insignificance.

On Christmas Eve I shall be thinking of you all very much, and I want you to believe that I too shall have a few hours of real joy and that I am not allowing my troubles to get the better of me. . . .

When one remembers the awful time so many are having in Berlin, it brings home to one more than anything else how much there is to be thankful for. It will certainly be a quiet Christmas for everybody, and the children will look back on it for long afterwards. But for the first time, perhaps, many will learn the true meaning of Christmas.

December 31st 1943

Christmas is over. It has brought me a few peaceful hours and revived many memories of the past. My gratitude for your preservation—and of the whole family—in the heavy air raids and my confidence of seeing you all again in the not too distant future was greater than all my troubles. I lit the candles you and M. sent me and read the Christmas story and a few beautiful carols and hummed them over to myself. This helped me to think of you all and to hope that you all might enjoy an hour or two of quietness after all the turbulence of the past weeks.

The New Year too will bring many anxieties and disturbances, though I believe we may on this New Year's Eve sing with greater confidence that verse from the New Year's hymn:

> *Shut fast the doors of woe,*
> *In every place let flow*
> *The streams of joy and peace,*
> *That bloodshed now may cease.*

I know no greater prayer or wish than that.

January 14th 1944

. . . I am sitting by the open window with the sunshine streaming in almost like spring. I take it for a good omen, this lovely beginning of the year. Compared to last year with all its troubles, this year can only be better.—I am getting on all right. I find it easier to concentrate, and am enjoying Dilthey very much indeed. . . .

February 20th 1944

Forgive me for not writing regularly for the past few weeks. I had hoped to have some definite news about my case, so I put off writing from day to day. They once told me quite definitely that everything would be settled by July 1943, then, as you yourselves will remember, it was to be September at the very latest. But now it is dragging on from month to month and nothing seems to happen. I'm quite sure that if they only got down to business the whole thing would be

[60

cleared up without any difficulty. And to think of all that is waiting outside for me to do! However hard I try to be patient and understanding, I sometimes feel it is better not to write any letters, but to keep silent. For in the first place my disordered thoughts and feelings would only give birth to wrong words, and secondly what I write would be very much out of date by the time it reached its destination. It costs no little effort to keep soberly to the facts, to banish illusions and fancies from my head and to content myself with things as they are. For where the external causes are shrouded in mystery one cannot help feeling that there must be some interior and invisible cause at work. Moreover our generation can no longer expect as yours could a life which finds full scope in professional and private activities, and thus achieve perfection and poise. And to make matters worse, we have the example of your life still before our eyes, which makes us painfully aware of the fragmentariness of our own. Yet this very fragmentariness points towards a fulfilment beyond the limits of human achievement. That is something which the death of so many of my pupils has brought home to me with particular force. Even though our lives may be blown to bits by the pressure of events as our houses are by the bombs, yet we should still have a glimpse of the way in which the whole was planned and conceived, and of what material we were building with or should have used had we lived.

March 3rd 1944

I daresay you have heard from M. how I said last time that our rations had been cut, a subject which we hardly ever mention. This makes us rather short of food, and I sometimes get rather hungry. This however may be partly due to the fact that I had a touch of the 'flu a few days ago and hardly felt like eating anything. Once more however you have come to the rescue, and I must frankly admit that the world looks quite a different place on a full stomach, and that it makes work easier too. All the same, I should hate to think I was depriving you of food when you have so much to do all day and need

61]

your strength more urgently than I. Now March has come again, and you have still not got away for a holiday.

I have been reading Harnack's history of the Prussian Academy. In some ways it makes enjoyable reading, but at times it's rather depressing. There are so few nowadays who have any real interest or sympathy for the nineteenth century. Contemporary music draws its inspiration from the sixteenth and seventeenth centuries, theology from the Reformation, philosophy from St. Thomas Aquinas and Aristotle, while the fashionable *Weltanschauung* seeks to return to the Teutonic past. Hardly anyone has the slightest idea what was achieved during the last century by our own grandfathers. How much of what they knew has already been forgotten! I believe people will one day be utterly amazed at the fertility of that age, now so much despised and so little known.

Could you please get hold of Dilthey's *Weltanschauung und Analyse des Menschen seit Renaissance und Reformation* for me?

April 26th 1944

This is my second spring in prison, but a very different one from last year. Then all my impressions were still fresh and vivid, and both hardships and joys were felt more keenly. Since then something has happened which I should never have thought possible—I have got used to it. The only thing that puzzles me is, which has been greater, the growth of insensitivity or the clarification of experience? It probably varies in different connexions. The things we get insensitive to are soon forgotten, since they are but trivial, whereas the things we have consciously or unconsciously assimilated will never be forgotten. Intense experience forges them into certainties, convictions and plans for the future, so that they become important for after-life. There is all the difference in the world between a month in prison and a whole year. A year brings not only interesting and intense impressions, but opens up a wholly new and far-reaching sphere of life. At the same time I am sure it requires certain interior presuppositions in order to be able to assimilate this particular aspect of life, and I think that

[62

a long confinement is extremely dangerous for the very young, as far as their spiritual development is concerned. The impressions of prison life are so overwhelming that they threaten to throw a good deal over board.—I must thank you for the comfort you give me by your continual visits, letters and parcels, and for the joy your greetings give me. It never palls, and each time I am encouraged afresh to use my time here to the full. Could you try and get hold of Ortega y Gasset's new book, *The Nature of Historical Crises,* and if possible his earlier work, *History as a System,* and also H. Pfeffer's *Das Britische Empire und die U.S.A.*? Let's hope we shall meet again soon!

With all good wishes,

Your grateful

Dietrich

V

Letters to a Friend,
Poems and Miscellaneous Papers

November 18th 1943

As you are in the neighbourhood, I am taking this opportunity of writing to you. You know of course that I am not even allowed to have a clergyman to see me. . . . So let me tell you what you ought to know about me. For the first twelve days I was segregated as a dangerous criminal and treated as one, and even to this day the cells each side of me are occupied by men in handcuffs awaiting death. During this time Paul Gerhardt was a wonderful help, more than I could have dreamed. So were the psalms and the Apocalypse. They helped to preserve me from any serious spiritual trial. You are the only person in the world who knows how often I have nearly given way to *accidie, tristitia*, with all its damaging effects on the soul. I feared at the time that you must be worrying about me on that account. But I told myself from the beginning that I wasn't going to oblige either the devil or man—they would just have to lump it—and I hope I shall always stick to my determination. At first I wondered a great deal whether it was really for the cause of Christ that I was giving you all this heart-break, but I soon put that out of my head as a temptation, and made up my mind that it was my duty to face the worst. In this way I became quite content about it all, and have remained so until this day (1 Peter 2.20; 3.14).

I was annoyed that I had not had time to finish my *Ethics* (it is probably confiscated for the time being), and it was some comfort to know I had told you the essentials, and even if you have forgotten what I told you it will doubtless emerge again in some shape or form. My ideas were still in a raw state, anyhow.

I was also disappointed not to be able to receive the sacrament with you, as I had hoped for a long time . . . but I

[64

know that although we have not been able to receive it physically, we have done so spiritually, and for that we may be glad and contented. But I did just want to tell you so.

I have been reading the Bible every day, and as soon as it was possible I started on some non-theological work. I have read the Old Testament through two and a half times, and have learnt a great deal. Then I began an essay on the subject of *Zeitgefühl* (the feeling of time) as an attempt to sort out my memories of my own past in a situation in which time might so easily seem to be empty and wasted. But more of that later.

Then I started on a bold enterprise that I have been thinking of for a long time, the story of a contemporary middle class family. The background for this was our frequent conversations on the subject and my own personal experiences. In short, it was to be a rehabilitation of middle class life as we have known it in our own families, and especially in the light of the Christian religion. It runs something like this. There are two families friendly with one another living in a small town. As their children grow up they gradually enter into the responsibilities of official positions, and they try to work together for the good of the community in their several capacities—mayor, doctor, parson, teacher, and engineer. You will recognize many familiar traits, and you come into it too. But I haven't got much further than the beginning, largely because my hopes of release have been continually disappointed, which has made it difficult for me to concentrate. But it gives me a great deal of pleasure. Only I wish I could talk it over with you every day. I miss that more than you think. . . .

As well as this I have written an essay on 'Speaking the Truth', and at the moment I am trying to compile some prayers for use in prison. It's strange there don't seem to be any in existence. I hope to have them distributed at Christmas.

And now for my reading. It is a great pity we never read any Stifter together; it would have been a great help for us in our talks. We shall have to put it off till later. But I have quite a lot to tell you about him. I wonder when! I have made my will and given it to my solicitor, in case the worst should happen, though I should not be surprised if you are in greater danger than I am. I shall be thinking of you every day, and praying God to keep you safe, and bring you home again. . . . I wonder whether, supposing I am acquitted and released, and I had to join up, there is any chance of my getting into your regiment? That would be wonderful! But don't worry about me at all if I should be condemned—one never knows what may happen. It does not worry me at all, except that I should have to sit here a few months awaiting my execution, which would not be pleasant. But then there is a good deal that is not pleasant! The charge on which I would be condemned is so unobjectionable that I should actually be proud of it. Still, I hope that if God preserves us we shall at least be able to spend Easter together and enjoy ourselves together once more. . . .

Let us however promise to remain true and pray for one another. I shall pray that you may be given strength and health, patience and protection through all trials and temptations—and you must make the same prayer for me. And if it should be decided that we never meet again, let us remember one another to the end with thoughts of gratitude and forgiveness—and may God grant that we may stand together before his throne one day, praying for one another and joining together in praise and thanksgiving.

. . . My greatest difficulty here (I think it would be yours too) seems to be getting up in the morning (see Jeremiah 31.26!). I am praying now quite simply for my release. There is a false kind of inertia which is quite un-Christian. We Christians need not be ashamed of showing a little impatience, longing and discontent with an unnatural fate, nor with a considerable amount of longing for freedom, earthly happiness and opportunity for work. We agree about that too, I am sure.

Well, in spite of, or rather because of, all we are going through, each of us in his own way, we shall still be the same as of old, shan't we? I hope you don't think I'm going to pieces here—I was never in less danger of that. And I believe the same applies to you. Won't it be a happy day when we can exchange experiences! I often get furious at not being free yet.

[66

PRAYERS FOR FELLOW PRISONERS

Christmas 1943

MORNING PRAYERS

O God,
Early in the morning do I cry unto thee.
Help me to pray,
And to think only of thee.
I cannot pray alone.

In me there is darkness,
But with thee there is light.
I am lonely, but thou leavest me not.
I am feeble in heart, but thou leavest me not.
I am restless, but with thee there is peace.
In me there is bitterness, but with thee there is patience;
Thy ways are past understanding, but
Thou knowest the way for me.

O heavenly Father,
I praise and thank thee
For the peace of the night.
I praise and thank thee for this new day.
I praise and thank thee for all thy goodness
and faithfulness throughout my life.
Thou hast granted me many blessings:
Now let me accept tribulation
from thy hand.
Thou wilt not lay on me more
than I can bear.
Thou makest all things work together for good
for thy children.

Lord Jesus Christ
Thou wast poor
and in misery, a captive and forsaken as I am.
Thou knowest all man's distress;
Thou abidest with me
when all others have deserted me;
Thou doest not forget me, but seekest me.
Thou willest that I should know thee and
turn to thee.
Lord, I hear thy call and follow thee;
Do thou help me.

O Holy Spirit,
Grant me the faith that will protect me from
despair: deliver me from the lusts of the flesh.
Pour into my heart such love for thee and for men,
that all hatred and bitterness may be blotted out.
Grant me the hope that will deliver me from fear
and timidity.

O Holy, merciful God,
my Creator and Redeemer,
my Judge and my Saviour,
Thou knowest me and all that I do.
Thou hatest and dost punish evil without respect of persons
in this world and the next.
Thou forgivest the sins of them
that heartily pray for forgiveness,
Thou lovest goodness and rewardest it on this earth
with a clear conscience, and in the world to come
with the crown of righteousness.

Chiefly do I remember all my loved ones,
my fellow-prisoners, and all who
in this house perform their hard service.
Lord have mercy.
Restore me to liberty,
and enable me so to live now,
that I may answer before thee and before the world.

[68

Lord, whatever this day may bring,
Thy Name be praised.
Amen.

★　　★　　★

In my sleep He watches yearning
and restores my soul
so that each recurring morning
love and goodness make me whole.
Were God not there,
his face not near,
He had not led me out of fear.
All things have their time and sphere:
God's love lasts for ever.

(Paul Gerhardt)

EVENING PRAYERS

O Lord my God, I thank thee that thou
hast brought this day to a close;
I thank thee that thou hast given me peace
in body and in soul.
Thy hand has been over me and has protected
and preserved me,
Forgive my puny faith,
the ill that I this day have done,
and help me to forgive all who
have wronged me.

Grant me a quiet night's sleep beneath
thy tender care.
And defend me from all the temptations
of darkness.

Into thy hands I commend my loved ones,
and all who dwell in this house;
I commend my body and soul.

O God, thy holy Name be praised.
Amen.

★   ★   ★

Each day tells the other
my life is but a journey
to great and endless life.
O sweetness of eternity
may my heart grow to love thee:
my home is not in time's strife.

(*Tersteegen*)

PRAYERS IN TIME OF DISTRESS

O Lord God,
Great is the misery that has come upon me;
My cares would overwhelm me,
I know not what to do.
O God, be gracious unto me and help me.
Grant me strength to bear what thou dost send,
and let not fear rule over me.
As a loving Father, take care of my loved ones
My wife and children.

O merciful God, forgive me all
the sins I have committed against thee,
and against my fellowmen.
I trust in thy grace, and commit my
life wholly into thy hands,
Do with me as seemeth best to thee, and as
is best for me.
Whether I live or die, I am with thee,
and thou art with me, my God.
Lord, I wait for thy salvation,
and for thy Kingdom.
Amen.

★   ★   ★

Every Christian in his place
should be brave and free,
with the world face to face,
Though death strikes, his spirit should
persevere, without fear
calm and good.
For death cannot destroy
but from grief brings relief
and opens gates to joy.
Closed the door of bitter pain,
bright the way where we may
all heaven gain.

(Paul Gerhardt)

LETTERS TO A FRIEND

November 20th 1943

If I should still be here over Christmas, don't worry about me. I should not really be frightened about it. A Christian can keep Christmas even in prison, more easily than family occasions, anyhow. My special thanks for getting permission to visit me. I am not expecting any complications this time. I didn't dare to ask you to do anything about it. I only hope it will come off this time. But you know that even if it is refused at the last moment, there is still the joy of thinking that you have tried, and it will only serve to make us more angry with certain people[1] for the time being (I sometimes think I don't get nearly angry enough over the whole business). So if it comes to that, let us swallow even that bitter pill, for after all we have been gradually getting used to such things in the past few months. I'm so glad I saw you just when I was arrested, and I shall never forget it.

Just one more point—about my daily routine. I get up at the same time as you do, and my day lasts till eight in the evening. I wear out my trousers sitting down while you wear out your soles running about. I read the *Voelkischer Beobachter* and the *Reich*, and I've got to know some *very* nice people.

[1] Dr. Roeder.

Every day they take me for half an hour's exercise, and in the afternoon they are giving me treatment for my rheumatism—I must say, they are very gentle with me, but it doesn't seem to do me much good. Once a week I get the most wonderful food parcels from you. Many thanks for them, and also for the cigars and cigarettes you sent me when you were away. I only hope you get your fill—are you often hungry? That would be too awful for words. There is nothing I miss here, except all of you. I wish you and I could play the G minor sonata and sing some Schütz together, and you could read to me Psalms 70 and 47. They were the best you ever did!

My cell is being spring cleaned. During the operations I am able to give the cleaner something to eat. One of them was sentenced to death the other day—that was a shock for me. In seven and a half months there is plenty to see, and especially one notices the tremendous consequences which may follow trivial acts of folly. I think a lengthy confinement is demoralizing for the bulk of the prisoners. I have been thinking out an alternative penal system, the principle of which is that everybody should be punished in the sphere in which his crime was committed: e.g. for absence without leave, the cancelling of all leave; for unlawful wearing of medals, longer service at the front; for robbing other soldiers, the temporary wearing of a label stating that the man is a thief; for blackmarketing, the reduction of rations, etc. Why is it that the Old Testament never punishes a man by depriving him of his liberty?

November 21st 1943

To-day is Remembrance Sunday . . . and after it comes Advent, with all its happy memories for you and me. . . . Life in a prison cell reminds me a great deal of Advent—one waits and hopes and potters about, but in the end what we do is of little consequence, for the door is shut, and it can only be opened from the outside. This idea has just occurred to me. But you must not think that we go in for symbolism very much here! And there are other things I have to tell you

[72

which may perhaps surprise you. One thing is that I do miss sitting down to table with others. The presents you send me acquire here a sacramental value; they remind me of the times we have sat down to table together. Perhaps the reason why we attach so much importance to sitting down to table together is that table fellowship is one of the realities of the Kingdom of God. Another thing is that I have found great help in Luther's advice that we should start our morning and evening prayers by making the sign of the cross. There is something objective about it, and that is what I need very badly here. Don't worry, I shan't come out of here a *homo religiosus*! On the contrary my suspicion and horror of religiosity are greater than ever. I often think of how the Israelites never uttered the name of God. I can understand that much better than I used to.

I am finding Tertullian, Cyprian and others of the Fathers extremely interesting. In some ways they are more relevant to our age than the Reformers, and another thing about them is that they provide a common platform between Protestants and Catholics.

. . . With regard to my case, I am convinced on purely legal grounds that my condemnation is out of the question.

November 22nd 1943

. . . Tell me how do you get on with the soldiers with your determination to take no notice of false accusations? Several times here I have given someone a dressing down for being impertinent, and they were so flabbergasted that they haven't given me any trouble since. I enjoy this sort of thing, but I know I oughtn't to be so sensitive about it. It makes me furious to see people who are unable to defend themselves being rebuked and sworn at. This streak of sadism in some people gets me worked up for hours on end. . . . The *Neues Lied*, which I got only a day or two ago, has brought back hosts of pleasant memories. You see, I am always thinking of things I want to talk over with you, and having begun again after all this long time I find it difficult to stop! . . .

November 23rd 1943

Last night's raid wasn't exactly pleasant. I was thinking of you all the time. At such moments prison life is no joke. I do hope you will be going back to S. again. It surprised me last night to see how nervous some of the soldiers who have come straight from the front line were while the alarm was on.

November 24th 1943

After yesterday's raid I think it is only right that I should let you know what arrangements I have made in case of my death. . . . I hope you will read this with your usual absence of sentimentality.

Friday, November 26th 1943

So it really came off! True, it was all too brief, but that does not matter. Even an hour or two wouldn't be enough. After we have been cut off from the world here for so long, we become so receptive that even a few minutes gives us food for thought for a long time after. I shall often think of how the four people who are my nearest and dearest were here with me. When I got back to my cell afterwards I paced up and down for a whole hour, while my dinner lay waiting for me on the table until it got quite cold, and in the end it made me laugh when I caught myself saying from time to time, 'How wonderful it was!' I never like calling anything 'indescribable', for it is a word you hardly ever need use if you take the trouble to express yourself clearly, but at the moment that's just what this morning seems to be. Karl's[1] cigar is on the table before me, and that's something really indescribable! Wasn't it kind and thoughtful of him!—and of V.[2] How grand it was that you saw them. And they are my favourite Wolf cigars from Hamburg, which I used to love so in better times. And beside me on a box there is the Advent crown, and your gigantic eggs on the shelf, which will provide my breakfast for several days

---

[1] Barth.   [2] Visser 't Hooft.

to come. It's no good my saying you ought not to have deprived yourselves of them, but that's what I think, though I am glad of them all the same. I can well remember the first time I ever visited a prison—it was when I went to see Fritz Onnasch, and you came with me. I'm afraid I took it very badly, though Fritz was wonderfully cheerful and nice. I do hope you didn't take it so badly when you came here to-day. It would be quite wrong to think that prison life is just uninterrupted torture. Far from it. And visits like yours relieve it for days on end, even if they do stir up long forgotten memories. But that doesn't do any harm either. It reminds me once more how many blessings I had, and gives me new hope and resolution. *Many* thanks, both to yourself and all the others.

November 27th 1943

Meanwhile, we have had the long awaited attack on Borsig. It was quite strange to see those flares which the leading aircraft dropped, just like a Christmas tree, coming down straight over my head. The cries of the prisoners in their cells were terrible. We had no dead, only injured, but it took us to one o'clock to get them all bandaged up. Immediately afterwards I was able to drop off in a sound sleep. People are talking quite openly about how terrified they were. I don't quite know what to make of it. Surely terror is something we ought to be ashamed of, something we ought not to talk about except in confession, otherwise it is bound to involve a certain amount of exhibitionism. On the other hand naïve frankness can be utterly disarming. Yet there is also a cynical, I might almost say ungodly, kind of frankness, the kind generally associated with drunkenness and whoredom, which is a sign of chaos. I am inclined to think that terror is one of the pudenda, one of the things that ought to be concealed. I must think about it further, and I have no doubt you have got your own ideas on the subject. Life in wartime is grim enough, but if we manage to live through it, we shall certainly have something on which to reconstruct international society, both materially and spiritually, on Christian principles. So we must try and store up these memories in our minds, allowing them to bear fruit, and not frittering them away. Never have we been so conscious of the wrath of an angry God, and that is in itself a sign of his grace. 'To-day if you will hear his voice, harden not your hearts.' The tasks before us are tremendous, but we must prepare ourselves for them now, so that we may be ready when they come.

November 28th 1943

Advent Sunday.—It began with a peaceful night. As I lay in bed yesterday evening I looked up our favourite Advent hymns in the *Neues Lied* for the first time. I can hardly hum any of them over to myself without thinking of Finkenwalde, Schlönwitz and Sigurdshof.[1] Early this morning I held my Sunday service, hung up the Advent crown on a nail, and fastened Lippi's picture of the Nativity in the middle of it. For breakfast I ate the second of your ostrich eggs—I just loved it! Soon after that I was fetched from my cell for an examination which lasted until noon. The recent air raids have brought a series of calamities—a land mine 25 yards away, the windows and the lights all shattered, the prisoners screaming for help and no one taking any notice of it apart from ourselves, though there was little we could do in the darkness, and one has to be cautious in opening the cell doors of the worst criminals, for you never know when they will hit you on the head with the leg of a chair and try to make a getaway. All things considered, it was not very nice! It made me spend some time after the raid writing out a report, stressing the importance of having first aid equipment available during air raids. I hope it will do some good. I am only too glad to be able to make some contribution to the general welfare, however small, particularly when my suggestions are likely to be appreciated.

By the way, I forgot to tell you that I smoked the Wolf cigar in the guardroom yesterday afternoon during a pleasant conversation. Its aroma was marvellous—many thanks for it.

[1] Preachers' Seminaries set up by the Confessing Church in Pomerania.

Since the raids started the cigarette situation has become calamitous. While they were being bandaged, the injured asked for a cigarette, and the medical orderlies and I had already used up a lot beforehand. So I am all the more grateful for what you brought with you the day before yesterday. Nearly every window in the place has been blown out, and the men are sitting frozen in their cells. I had actually forgotten to open my windows as I left the cell, yet they were quite undamaged. I'm glad about it, though it makes me terribly sorry for the others. How marvellous that you are home for Advent! I can imagine you singing hymns together for the first time just at this very moment. It makes me think of the Altdorfer Nativity and the verse:

> *The crib glistens bright and clear;*
> *The night brings in a new light here.*
> *Darkness now must fade away,*
> *For faith within the light must stay.*

and also the Advent melody:

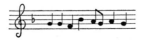

though not in the usual four four time, but in the swinging expectant rhythm which suits the text so much better. After this I am going to read another of H. W. Riehl's amusing tales. You would find them great fun too, and they are just the thing for reading out aloud to the family. You must try and get hold of them some time.

November 29th 1943

This Monday is quite unique. Usually on a Monday morning the shouting and swearing in the corridors is at its worst, but after the experiences of last week even the noisiest ones have become subdued, a change one cannot help noticing! Now something which will particularly interest you. During

these heavy air raids, and especially the last one, the windows
were blown out by the land mine, and bottles and medical
supplies from the shelves and cupboards fell to the ground.
All this time I lay in complete darkness on the floor, with little
hope of coming through it all safely. Now here's the point—
it led me back to prayer and to the Bible just like a child. More
of that later when I see you. In more than one respect my
confinement is acting like a wholesome though drastic cure.
But I can only tell you the details when we meet again. . . .
Roeder[1] was too sure he would get his own own way with
me at first, and now he must content himself with a charge
which is so utterly absurd, that it will reflect very little to his
credit.

In the last month or two I have learnt for the first time in
my life how much comfort and help I get from others. . . .
We often want to do everything ourselves, but that is a mark of
false pride. Even what we owe to others belongs to ourselves,
and is a part of our own lives. And when we want to calculate
just how much we have learnt ourselves and how much we
owe to others, it is not only un-Christian, but useless. What we
are in ourselves, and what we owe to others makes us a complete whole. I wanted to tell you this because I've only just
found it out, though not really for the first time, for we have
realized it implicitly all through the years of our *vita communis*.

Advent II

I so much want to spend a quiet Sunday morning talking
things over with you, that I am writing this letter, though
I don't know whether it will reach you, and if so, how or
where. I wonder where we shall both be for Christmas, and
what sort of a Christmas it will be. I hope you succeed in
conveying something of its joy to your fellow-soldiers.
For joy and contentment can be just as infectious as fear
and panic. I am sure such a spirit can give us immense
moral authority, provided we are not just showing off, but
are quite genuine and sincere. Men need a fixed pole they can

[1] Legal adviser to the military authorities, and Chief Investigation Officer.

look to for direction. I don't think either of us are the sort that like showing off, though that has nothing to do with the courage which comes from the grace of God.

My thoughts and feelings seem to be getting more and more like the Old Testament, and no wonder, I have been reading it much more than the New for the last few months. It is only when one knows the ineffability of the Name of God that one can utter the name of Jesus Christ. It is only when one loves life and the world so much that without them everything would be gone, that one can believe in the resurrection and a new world. It is only when one submits to the law that one can speak of grace, and only when one sees the anger and wrath of God hanging like grim realities over the head of one's enemies that one can know something of what it means to love them and forgive them. I don't think it is Christian to want to get to the New Testament too soon and too directly. We have often talked about this before, and I am more than ever convinced that I am right. You cannot and must not speak the last word before you have spoken the next to last. We live on the next to last word, and believe on the last, don't we? Lutherans (so-called) and pietists would be shocked at such an idea, but it is true all the same. In my *Cost of Discipleship* I just hinted at this (in Chap. I), but did not carry it any further. I must do so some day. The consequences are far-reaching, e.g. for the problem of Catholicism, for the doctrine of the ministry, for the use of the Bible, etc., and above all for ethics. Why is it that in the Old Testament men lie so frequently and on such a grand scale to the glory of God (I have collected together all the instances), that they commit murder, trickery, robbery, adultery and even whoredom (see the genealogy of Jesus), that they doubt, blaspheme and curse, whereas there is no sign of these things in the New Testament? It's easy to say that the Old Testament represents an earlier stage of religious evolution, but that is too naïve, for after all it is the same God in both Testaments. We shall have to talk about this further when we meet again!

In the meantime evening has come. I was brought back just now from the guardroom to my abode by a corporal, who just as he left said to me with an embarrassed smile, but quite seriously, 'Pray for us, Padre, that we may be spared an alarm to-night.'

For some time I have been taking my daily exercise in the company of a fellow who has been a District Orator, Regional Leader, and a Government Director, as well as a former member of the Governing Body of the German-Christian Church in Brunswick, and is at present a leader of the party in Warsaw. He has gone completely to pieces here, and clings to me like a child, consulting me about the slightest trivialities, informing me each time he has cried, etc. After snubbing him for several weeks, I am now trying to administer a little comfort, for which he is touchingly grateful, telling me again and again how glad he is to have met someone like me here. In short, one is confronted here with the strangest situations—if only I could tell you properly about them!

I have been thinking over what I said in a recent letter about my own fear. I am inclined to think that in this matter we are all too prone to pretend to be honest and 'natural' over something which is really a symptom of sin. In fact, it is just like talking openly about sex. It is not always 'honest' to reveal secrets. It was God who made clothes for men, which means that *in statu corruptionis* there are many things in human life which ought to be kept covered over, and evil at any rate ought to be left concealed if it is too early to eradicate it. To uncover is the mark of cynicism, and when the cynic prides himself on his honesty and pretends to be an enthusiast for truth, he overlooks the really important point that since the fall reticence and secrecy are essential. In my opinion the greatness of Stifter lies in his refusal to poke and pry into the insides of men, that he respects the need of reticence, and is content to observe men cautiously from the outside. He has no room for unhealthy curiosity. I remember Frau K. once telling me how shocked she was at a slow motion film showing the growth of plant life. She and her husband both found it more than they could stand; they thought there was something indecent in prying like this into the secret of life. Stifter takes a very similar line. Yet may this not be dangerously akin to

[80

what we in this country call 'English hypocrisy', which we contrast with 'German honesty'? I believe we Germans have never properly understood the meaning of reticence, and that means in the last resort that we have not understood the *status corruptionis* of the world. Somewhere in his *Anthropology* Kant makes the shrewd observation that the man who ignores outward appearances and repudiates everything external is a traitor against humanity.

By the way was it you who got hold of the *Witiko* which was brought to me on Friday? Who else could it have been? Although I think it is more painstaking than brilliant, much of it interests me a great deal. Many thanks.

I have been writing an essay on 'Speaking the Truth'. By that I mean saying what actually is, that is, shewing respect for secrecy, intimacy and concealment. 'Betrayal' is not truth any more than flippancy, cynicism, etc. Secrecy may only be revealed in confession, that is, in the presence of God. More about that later too!

There are two ways of dealing with adversity. One way, the easier, is to ignore it altogether. I have got about as far as that. The other and more difficult way is to face up to it and triumph over it. I can't manage that yet, but I must learn to do it, for the first way is really a slight, though I believe permissible, piece of self-deception.

December 15th 1943

When I read your letter yesterday I felt as though the sources of my intellectual life, which were beginning to dry up, had started to trickle again. No doubt that will strike you as exaggerated, though it's perfectly true. For secluded as I am, I have no other alternative but to live wholly on the past. . . . My thoughts had grown rusty and tired during recent weeks, but now your letter has set them going again. After being so used to talking everything over with you, the sudden and prolonged interruption means a profound change and a tremendous hardship. Now at last we are in communication again. . . . Roeder and Co. have smashed up so much china already that we must not let them destroy our personal relationships, which are the most important things in our lives. . . . And now I am taking up your 'fireside chat', which gives me great pleasure. (Appropriately enough the electricity has just failed again, and I am sitting by candlelight). I can imagine us sitting together as we used to in the old days after supper (and after our regular evening's work)[1] upstairs in my room, smoking, occasionally strumming a tune on the piano and discussing the day's events. I should have no end of questions to ask, about your training, about your journey to Karolus.[2] . . . And then at last I would start telling you that despite everything I have written so far, everything here is too awful for words. I should tell you how my grim experiences often follow me into the night, and the only way I can shake them off is by reciting one hymn after another, and that when I wake up it is generally with a sigh, rather than a hymn of praise. It is possible to get used to physical hardships, and to live for months out of the body so to speak—in fact it is almost too easy, but one can never get used to the psychological strain. On the contrary I feel somehow that everything I see and hear is putting years on me, and making life a loathsome burden. Perhaps you are surprised at my talking like this after all my letters. You wrote very nicely that 'it was costing me no little effort' to reassure you about my situation. I often ask myself who I really am. Am I the man who keeps squirming under these ghastly experiences in abysmal misery? Or am I the man who keeps scourging himself and outwardly pretends to others (and to himself as well) that he is a contented, cheerful easy-going fellow, and expects everyone to admire him for it? I mean, admire him for putting up this theatrical show, for that is what it really is. What does self-control really mean? In short I know less than ever about myself, and am getting more and more bored with psychology and fed up with introspective analysis. That is probably what has made Stifter such a help to me. There is something more at stake than self-knowledge.

Then I would ask you whether you think that this trial,

[1] Listening to foreign broadcasts.　　　[2] Karl Barth.

[82

which has brought to light my connexion with the resistance group inside Canaris's Security Branch (for I can hardly think that has remained a secret) will stop me from taking up my ministry again later on? These are things which at the moment I can only discuss with you, and perhaps we shall be able to talk about it together if you are given permission to see me. Please think it over and tell me the truth.

. . . I often feel as though the best part of my life was already past, and that all I have to do now is to finish my *Ethics*. Yet you know, when I feel like this there comes over me an unimaginable longing not to quit this life without leaving some traces behind me, a wish that seems more redolent of the Old Testament than of the New. . . . If only I could see you as a free man before you leave! But if it is now their intention to keep me here over Christmas, I shall face it my own way like a Christmas in the front line, so you needn't worry about that. Great battles are easier to fight and less wearing than daily skirmishes. And I also hope you will manage to get a few days' leave in February—I shall certainly be out of here by then. For in spite of all the nonsense they are charging me with they are bound to let me out when the time is up.

I am re-writing my essay on 'Speaking the Truth', and trying to draw a sharp contrast between confidence, loyalty and secrecy on the one hand and the cynical conception of truth, for which all these obligations do not exist, on the other. Lying is destructive and inimical to reality as it is in God. The man who tells the truth out of cynicism is a liar.—By the way, it is remarkable how little I miss going to church. I wonder why.

Your reference to the Biblical image of 'eating the letter' is very much to the point.—If you manage to get to Rome, do visit Sch. in the *Propaganda Fide*!—Have you found the tone among the troops very bad, or do they show you some respect? Here in the guard room the men are certainly coarse, but not churlish. Some of the younger prisoners seem to have suffered so much under the strain of solitary confinement and the long evenings in the dark that they have completely gone to pieces. That is another idiotic thing, locking up these people here for months on end with nothing to do. It is demoralizing from every point of view.

December 18th 1943

You too must at least have a letter for Christmas. I have given up all hope of release. As far as I can see, I should have been set free on the 17th December, but the —— wanted to take the safest course, and now I shall probably sit here for weeks. The past weeks have been more of a strain than anything I have been through before. But it cannot be altered. It is always more difficult to adapt oneself to something which might have been altered than it is to the inevitable. But once facts have taken shape they must simply be accepted. What I am thinking of most to-day is that you too will soon be facing facts which will be really hard for you, probably harder than for me. I think we ought to do all in our power to alter these facts while there is still time, and then when all our efforts have proved fruitless it becomes much easier to endure them. Of course, not everything that happens is the will of God, yet in the last resort nothing happens without his will (Matthew 10.29), i.e. through every event, however untoward, there is always a way through to God. When a man has entered upon a supremely happy marriage for which he thanks God, it is an awful blow to discover that the same God now demands a period of such great privation. In my experience nothing tortures us so much as longing. There are many who have been shaken up so violently from the earliest days of their youth, that they are unable to put up with a protracted period of tension, and therefore contrive for themselves substitute pleasures which though short-lived offer readier satisfaction. That is the fate of the proletarian classes and the ruin of all intellectual fertility. It is not true to say that it is good for man to have gone through hard times in his early life. In most cases it is his downfall. True, it hardens them more for times like ours, but it also makes them infinitely less sensitive. When *we* are forcibly separated from those we love, we simply *cannot*, like so many others, contrive for ourselves some cheap substitute

[84

elsewhere.—I don't mean because of moral considerations, but because we are what we are. We find the very idea of substitutes repulsive. All we can do is to wait patiently; we must suffer the unutterable agony of separation, and feel the longing until it makes us sick. For that is the only way in which we can preserve our relationship with our loved ones unimpaired. There have been a few occasions in my life when I have had to learn what homesickness means. There is no agony worse than this, and during these months in prison I have sometimes been terribly homesick. And as I am sure you will have to go through the same agony during these coming months, I wanted to tell you what I had learnt from it in case it may be of some help to you. The first and invariable effect of such longing is an itching desire to abandon the daily routine, with the result that our lives become disordered. I used to be tempted sometimes to stay in bed after six in the morning, which would have been perfectly possible, and to sleep on. Up to now I have never succumbed to that temptation. I realized that that would have been the first stage of capitulation, and no doubt worse would have followed. A good piece of self-discipline is to do a daily dozen every morning and have a cold wash down, which is a real support to one's morale. There is nothing worse in such times than to try and find a substitute for the irreplaceable. It won't succeed anyhow, and can only lead to even greater indiscipline, for then the power to overcome tension, which can only come from looking the longing straight in the face, is used up, and endurance becomes even more intolerable.

. . . Another point, I am sure it is best not to talk to strangers about our feelings; that only makes matters worse, though we should always be ready to listen to the troubles of others. Above all, we must never give way to self-pity. And on the Christian aspect of the matter, there are some lines which say:

> . . . that we remember, what we would fain forget,
> That this poor earth is not our home

—a very important sentiment, though one which can only

come right at the end; for I am sure we ought to love God in our *lives* and in all the blessings he sends us. We should trust him in our lives, so that when our time comes, but not before, we may go to him in love and trust and joy. But, speaking frankly, to long for the transcendent when you are in your wife's arms is, to put it mildly, a lack of taste, and it is certainly not what God expects of us. We ought to find God and love him in the blessings he sends us. If he pleases to grant us some overwhelming earthly bliss, we ought not to try and be more religious than God himself. For then we should spoil that bliss by our presumption and arrogance; we should be letting our religious fantasies run riot and refusing to be satisfied with what he gives. Once a man has found God in his earthly bliss and has thanked him for it, there will be plenty of opportunities for him to remind himself that these earthly pleasures are only transitory, and that it is good for him to accustom himself to the idea of eternity, and there will be many hours in which he can say with all sincerity, 'I would that I were home'. But everything in its season, and the important thing is to keep step with God, and not get a step or two in front of him (nor for that matter, a step or two behind him either). It is arrogant to want to have everything at once—matrimonial bliss, and the cross, and the heavenly Jerusalem, where there is no longer marriage, nor giving in marriage. 'To everything there is a season' (Ecclesiastes 3). Everything has its time—'a time to weep and a time to laugh . . . a time to embrace, and a time to refrain from embracing . . . a time to rend, and a time to sew . . . and God seeketh again that which is passed away.' These last words mean that God gathers up again with us our past, which belongs to us. So when we are seized by a longing for the past—which may happen when we are least expecting it—we can always remind ourselves that that is but one of the many hours which God is holding ready for us. Hence we ought not to seek the past again by ourselves, but do so with God. Enough of this! I see I have attempted too much, for there is nothing I can tell you about these matters which you do not already know yourself.

Advent IV

. . . For the past week or two these words have been
constantly running through my head:

> *Let pass, dear brother, every pain;*
> *What lacketh you I'll bring again.*

What does 'bring again' mean? It means that nothing is lost,
everything is taken up again in Christ, though of course it is
transfigured in the process, becoming transparent, clear and
free from all self-seeking and desire. Christ brings it all again
as God intended it to be, without the distortion which results
from human sin. The doctrine of the restoration of all things—
ἀνακεφαλαίωσις—which is derived from Ephesians 1.10,
recapitulatio (Irenaeus), is a magnificent conception, and full of
comfort. This is the way in which the words 'God seeketh
again that which is passed away' are fulfilled. And no one has
expressed this more simply than Paul Gerhardt in the words
which he puts in the mouth of the Christ-child:

> *Ich bringe alles wieder.*[1]

Perhaps this line will help you during the coming weeks. I
have also learnt to appreciate for the first time in my life the
hymn 'Beside thy cradle here I stand'. I had never been able
to make much of it before. One needs to be alone for a long
time and to meditate upon it in order to appreciate it. Every
word is packed with meaning and beauty. It is a trifle mystical
in a monkish sort of way, though not unduly so. After all, it
is right to speak of 'I and Christ' as well as of 'we', and it
could hardly be better expressed than it is in this carol. There
are also a few passages in a similar vein in the *Imitation of
Christ*, which I am reading at random in the Latin original—
infinitely superior to the German translation. At times I think of

[1] From the hymn *Fröhlich soll mein Herze springen*.

87]

from the Augustinian *O bone Jesu* by Schütz. Is not this phrase, with its combination of ecstatic longing and transparent devotion, suggestive of the restoration of all earthly desire? Restoration of course must not be confused with sublimation, for sublimation is σάρξ (and pietistic?!), and restoration 'spirit', not in the sense of spiritualization, but as καινὴ κτίσις through the πνεῦμα ἅγιον, a new creation through the Holy Spirit. I believe that this point is also of great importance when we reply to those who ask us about their relation to their dead. 'I bring all again', that is we cannot and ought not to take them for ourselves, but allow Christ to give them back to us. By the way, at my funeral I should like the choir to sing: 'One thing of the Lord I will require', 'Make haste, O God, to help me' and 'O bone Jesu'.[1]

At midday on Christmas Eve a dear old fellow is coming here at his own suggestion to play some carols on a cornet. But some whose judgement I should rely on, say it only makes the prisoners unhappy and makes the day even harder for them to bear. 'It demoralizes them', said one, and I can well imagine it. In former years the prisoners used to start whistling and kicking up a row, no doubt to stop themselves from becoming sentimental. I am quite sure that in view of all the misery prevalent here it is no use giving them pretty-pretty, sentimental reminders of Christmas. It would be better if a good personal message or a sermon could be included in the programme. Without something of the kind music alone can be positively dangerous. Please don't think I am frightened of it myself, but I am sorry for all these helpless young soldiers in their cells. Nothing can really be done to relieve the depression here, and probably it is right that this should be so. I am giving a good deal of thought to a fundamental reform of the penal system, and hope to be able to offer some useful suggestions on the subject.

[1] All by Heinrich Schütz.

[88

If this letter reaches you in time, please try to get me something good to read over the Christmas season. I asked for some books a little while ago, but they do not seem to be forthcoming. I don't mind something exciting, if you like. And if you can lay your hands on Barth's *Doctrine of Predestination* or his *Doctrine of God*,[1] include them too. The propagandist who accompanies me on my daily walks is getting more and more unendurable. Most people here do at least try to keep themselves under control, but this fellow is a complete wreck, and cuts a really sorry figure. I try to be as nice to him as possible, and talk to him like a child. Sometimes he can be almost funny. What pleases me more, however, is to hear that when I am up in the guardroom the word goes round the kitchen or the garden, and the prisoners working there try to come up on some pretext or other to chat with me. Of course it is not really allowed, but I was pleased to hear about it, and you will be too. Only don't let it get around.—I shouldn't be surprised if this isn't the last uncensored letter I shall be able to write to you.

Must close now. Read Proverbs 18.24, and don't forget it.

December 22nd 1943

They seem to have made up their minds that I am not to be with you for Christmas, though nobody dares to tell me so. I wonder why. Do they think I am so easily upset? . . . The English have a very useful word for this sort of thing— they call it 'tantalizing' . . . I do want you to realize that I believe my attitude towards my case ought to be one of faith, whereas I am letting it become too much a matter of calculation and foresight. I am not really bothered about whether I shall be home for Christmas, for that is only a childish question. I am sure I could renounce that, if only I could do so in faith, knowing that it is inevitable. I can bear all things in faith (I hope so, anyhow), even my condemnation, and even the

[1] Church Dogmatics, Vol. II, Parts 1 and 2. These were banned in Germany at the time, and had to be sent from Switzerland without title or cover.

other consequences I fear (see Psalm 18.30): but anxious calculation wears one down. Don't worry if something worse befalls me [removal to a concentration camp]. Several of the other brethren have already been through that. But this shilly-shallying, this continual consultation without action, this refusal to face up to risks is positively dangerous. I must be able to know for certain that I am in the hands of God, and not in men's. Then everything can be easy, even the severest privations. There is no question of my being 'understandably impatient', as people are probably saying of me: what matters is that I should face everything in faith. . . .

You ought to know that I have not for a moment regretted coming home in 1939.[1] I knew quite well what I was about, and acted with a clear conscience. I have no desire to cross out of my life anything that has happened since, either in the world at large, or to me personally (Sigurdshof, East Prussia, Ettal, my illness, and all the help you gave me then, the time in Berlin, and my present confinement). And I regard my sitting here (do you remember how I prophesied last March what the coming year would bring?) as my own part in the fate of Germany. I look back on the past without any self-reproach, and accept the present in the same spirit. But I don't want to be unsettled by the machinations of men. We can only live in faith and assurance, you out there at the front, and I in my cell.—I have just come across this in the *Imitation of Christ: Custodi diligenter cellam tuam, et custodiet te* ('Look after your cell, and it will look after you'). May God keep the light of faith burning in our souls.

Christmas Eve 1943

It is half past nine in the evening; I have had a few lovely hours of peace and quiet, and have been happy to think that you two are able to spend this day together.

One of my greatest joys this Christmas is that we were able to keep up the tradition of exchanging the daily texts for the

[1] From America just before the outbreak of war, despite tempting invitations from his American friends.

ensuing year. I had already thought about it, and hoped we should manage it, though I was not at all sure whether we would. And now this little book, which has been such a great help to me in recent months, will be our constant companion in the New Year, and as we read it in the morning we shall think especially of one another. Many, many thanks.

I wish I could say something to help you in the time of separation which lies immediately ahead. There is no need to speak about its difficulties, but as I have learnt something about it myself during the last nine months, having been separated during that time from all those I love, I should like to pass it on to you.

In the first place nothing can fill the gap when we are away from those we love, and it would be wrong to try and find anything. We must simply hold out and win through. That sounds very hard at first, but at the same time it is a great consolation, since leaving the gap unfilled preserves the bonds between us. It is nonsense to say that God fills the gap: he does not fill it, but keeps it empty so that our communion with another may be kept alive, even at the cost of pain. In the second place the dearer and richer our memories, the more difficult the separation. But gratitude converts the pangs of memory into a tranquil joy. The beauties of the past are not endured as a thorn in the flesh, but as a gift precious for its own sake. We must not wallow in our memories or surrender to them, just as we don't gaze all the time at a valuable present, but get it out from time to time, and for the rest hide it away as a treasure we know is there all the time. Treated in this way, the past can give us lasting joy and inspiration. Thirdly, times of separation are not a total loss, nor are they completely unprofitable for our companionship—at least there is no reason why they should be. In spite of all the difficulties they bring, they can be a wonderful means of strengthening and deepening fellowship. Fourthly, it has been borne in upon me here with peculiar force that a concrete situation can always be mastered, and that only fear and anxiety magnify them to an immeasurable degree beforehand. From the moment we awake until we fall asleep we must commend our loved ones wholly and

91]

unreservedly to God and leave them in his hands, transforming our anxiety for them into prayers on their behalf.

'Tis vain to fret and fear
God will not therefore hear.

Christmas Day

. . . Once more all my marvellous Christmas presents are arranged on the edge of the tipped-up bed, and in front of me are the pictures which I enjoy so much. The memory of your visit gives me food for thought all the time. It was something I really couldn't do without. My longing to have someone to talk to is far worse than physical hunger. . . . A few pregnant remarks are enough to touch upon a wide range of questions and clear them up. This intimacy of ours took so many years to cultivate, not always without friction, and we must never lose it again. What a lot we touched on in that hour and a half, and how much we learnt from each other. I am so grateful to you for fixing up the meeting and bringing it off. . . . They have tried to do everything possible here to give me a pleasant Christmas, but I was glad to be alone again. I often wonder how I shall adapt myself to company again after this. You remember how I often used to retire to my room after some great celebration. I'm afraid I must have grown even worse, for despite all my privations I have come to love solitude. I enjoy a talk with one or two others, but I simply loathe any larger gathering, and anything in the nature of chatter or gossip I just cannot stand. . . .

January 23rd 1944

Since you left for the front on Jan. 9th my thoughts about you have taken a new shape. . . . That Sunday was just as bad a wrench for me as it was for you. It is a strange feeling to see a friend whose life has been bound up so intimately with your own for so many years going out to meet an unknown

[92

future which you can do practically nothing about. It makes
you feel so utterly helpless. There are however, it seems to
me, two sides to this helplessness. It brings both anxiety and
relief. For so long as we are able to influence another's life, we
can't help wondering whether what we are doing for him is
really for his best. But when every opportunity of interfering
with his life is cut off at a blow, you cannot help feeling that
however anxious you may be about him, his life has now been
placed in better and more powerful hands than your own. Our
greatest task during these coming weeks, and maybe months,
will be to trust in these hands. Whatever weakness, self-
reproach and guilt we contribute to these events, in the events
themselves is God. If we survive all this we shall be able to see
quite clearly that all has turned out for the best. The idea
that we could have avoided many of life's difficulties if
we had taken things more quietly is one that cannot be taken
seriously for a moment. As I look back on your past I am
sure that everything has turned out for the best, and so we
have every reason to hope that what is happening at the
present can only be for the best too. To renounce a full life
and all its joys in order to escape pain is neither Christian
nor human. . . .

The news of the Nettuno landing has just come in. Are you
anywhere thereabouts? When things like this happen I see how
hard it is for me to take things calmly: I can only do so at the
cost of repeated effort. In any case self-possession is only a
euphemism for indifference and indolence, so to that extent
it is not exactly a respectable thing! I was reading some
Lessing the other day, and came across this: 'I am too proud
to consider myself unlucky. Just grind your teeth and let your
canoe sail where the wind and the waves take it. Enough that
I have no intention of upsetting it myself.' Is such an attitude
to be forbidden to the Christian? Is it, for example, better for
him to be soft-hearted and to surrender prematurely? Is there
not a kind of self-possession which proudly grinds its teeth, but
is quite different from a dour, rigid, lifeless and unthinking
submission to the inevitable? I am sure we honour God more
if we gratefully accept the life he gives us with all its blessings,

loving it and drinking it to the full, grieving deeply and sincerely when we have belittled or thrown away any of the precious things of life (some people grumble at such behaviour and say it is bourgeois to be so weak and sensitive) than we do if we are insensitive towards the blessings of life, and therefore equally insensitive towards pain. Job's word, 'The Lord hath given . . .', etc., includes that rather than excludes it, as can be seen from the speeches he makes with so much gnashing of teeth, and from their justification by God (Chapter 42.7ff.) in face of the false, premature, pious submission of his friends.

I am much impressed by your remarks about friendship in this connexion. As compared with marriage and the ties of kindred, friendship has no generally recognized rights, and is therefore wholly dependent on its own inherent quality. It is by no means easy to classify friendship sociologically. Perhaps it is a subheading of culture and education, and brotherhood a subheading of Church, and comradeship a subheading of labour and politics. Marriage, labour, the state and the Church all exist by divine decree. But what of culture and education? I don't think they can be classified under labour, tempting though that may be from many points of view. They belong not to the sphere of obedience, but to that of freedom, which surrounds all three spheres of the divine decrees. The man who is ignorant of this sphere of freedom can be a good father, citizen and worker, and even a Christian, but hardly a complete man, and therefore hardly a good Christian in the widest sense of the term. Our Protestant (not Lutheran) Prussian world has been so dominated by the divine decrees, that it has allowed this sphere of freedom to be pushed into the background. It almost looks to-day as though the Church alone offers any prospect for the recovery of the sphere of freedom (art, education, friendship and play, 'æsthetic existence', as Kierkegaard called it). I am convinced of the truth of this, and it would help us to a new understanding of the Middle Ages. What man is there among us for instance who can give himself with an easy conscience to the cultivation of music, friendship, games or happiness? Surely not ethical man, but

[94

only the Christian. Just because friendship belongs to this sphere of freedom (the freedom of the Christian man?!) it must be confidently defended against all the disapproving frowns of moralism, though without claiming for it the *necessitas* of a divine decree, but only the *necessitas* of freedom! I believe that within the sphere of this freedom friendship is by far the rarest and most priceless treasure, for where else does it survive in this world of ours, dominated as it is by the three other decrees? It cannot be compared with the blessings of the decrees, for it is *sui generis*; its relation to them is that of the cornflower to the cornfield.

As regards what you said about Christ being afraid, it only comes out in prayer (as it does in the psalms). I have often wondered how the Evangelists came to record this prayer, which nobody can have heard. The suggestion that it must have been revealed by Jesus during the great forty days is only a subterfuge. Have you any explanation to offer?

Your reference to Socrates' remarks about culture and death may prove very valuable. I must give it further thought. The only thing I am clear about at the moment is that education which breaks down in face of danger is not education at all. A liberal education which will not enable us to face danger and death does not deserve the name. Education must be able to face death and danger—*impavidum ferient ruinae*, the ruins will strike the fearless man (Horace)—even if it cannot 'conquer' them; what does conquer mean? By finding forgiveness in judgement and joy in terror? We must discuss this further.

What will happen to Rome? I can't bear to think of its being destroyed. What a good thing we saw it in peacetime.

I am still getting on all right, working and waiting. Nothing has happened to shake my optimism, and I hope it is the same with you too. Goodbye, may we meet again soon!

If you happen to see the Laocoon again, see whether you do not think the head of the father provided the model for the later representations of Christ. Last time I saw this classical man of sorrows it impressed me deeply and kept me thinking for a long time.

I have had to take a new line with the companion of my daily walks. Although he has done his best to ingratiate himself with me, he said something about the Jews the other day, which made me more offhanded and cool to him than I have ever been to anyone before, and I have also seen to it that he has been deprived of certain little comforts. Now he feels himself obliged to go round whimpering for a while, but I haven't a scrap of pity for him. He is really a sorry figure, but certainly not poor Lazarus!

January 29th and 30th 1944

. . . and as I find it hard not to write to you, I am using this quiet Saturday afternoon, so different from the noise we have had these last two nights. I wonder how you have taken your baptism of fire, and your first encounter with our Anglo-Saxon opponents, whom we have met hitherto only in time of peace.

When I think of you every morning and evening I cannot get out of my mind all your cares and anxieties, instead of praying for you as I ought. That reminds me, I want to talk to you some day about prayer in time of trouble. It is a difficult matter, though our misgivings about it can hardly be good. In Psalm 50 we are told quite clearly: 'Call upon me in the time of trouble: so will I hear thee and thou shalt praise me.' The history of the children of Israel is one long story of such cries for help. And I must say, the experiences of the last two nights have reopened the problem for me in quite an elementary way. While the bombs are falling all round the building, I cannot help thinking of the divine judgement, of the outstretched arm of his wrath (Isaiah 5.25; 9.11-10.4), and of my own unpreparedness. It makes me feel how men can make vows, and then I think of you all and say, better me than one of them, and that reminds me how deeply I am attached to you. I won't say any more about it for the moment, for it's something that can only be discussed by word of mouth. But when all's said and done, it is true that it needs trouble to drive us to prayer, though every time I feel it is

[96

something to be ashamed of. Perhaps that is because up to now I have not had a chance of putting in a Christian word at such a moment. As we were all lying on the floor yesterday, someone muttered 'O God, O God'—he is normally a frivolous sort of chap—but I couldn't bring myself to offer him any Christian encouragement or comfort. All I did was to glance at my watch and say: 'It won't last any more than ten minutes now.' There was nothing premeditated about it; it came quite automatically, though perhaps I had a feeling that it was wrong to force religion down his throat just then. Incidentally, Jesus himself did not try to convert the two thieves on the cross; he waited until one of them turned to him.

I am sorry to say I suffered a sad loss the night before last. The most intelligent and to me the personally most attractive man here was killed in the city by a direct hit. I had intended to introduce him to you on some future occasion, and we had already planned to do things together in the future. We had a good many talks, and the other day he brought me *Daumier und die Justiz*, which I still have by me. He was a really educated man of working-class origin, a philosopher, and the father of three children. His death was an awful blow.

During the last day or two I have resumed the work I told you about before. It is about the meeting of two old friends after they had been parted for several years during the war. I hope to send it to you soon. You needn't worry, it won't be a best-seller!

In early days even one of our present problems would have been enough to take up all our time. Now we are required to bring to some common denominator such varied problems as war, marriage, the Church, profession, housing, the danger and death of our nearest and dearest, and as if all that were not enough, my imprisonment here. No doubt most people would regard these as quite separate problems, but for the Christian and the man of liberal education that is impossible: he cannot split up his life into water-tight compartments. The common denominator is to be sought both in thought and in practical living in an integrated attitude to life. The man who allows himself to be torn into fragments by events and problems has not passed the test for the present and the future. It is related in the story of young Witiko how he set out on life with the intention of doing everything there was to be done. In other words, it is a question of the ἄνθρωπος τέλειος (the primary meaning of τέλειος is 'whole', 'complete')—'Ye therefore shall be perfect (τέλειος), as your heavenly Father is perfect' (Matthew 5.48), in contrast to the ἀνὴρ δίψυχος the 'double minded man' of James 1.8. Witiko does everything there is to be done by adapting himself to the realities of life, by always listening to the advice of others more experienced than himself, thus showing himself a member of the 'whole'. We can never achieve this wholeness on our own; it can only be acquired with the help of others.

I have just started Harnack's *History of the Prussian Academy*, and it's first rate. I am sure he put his heart and soul into this book, and more than once he said he thought it was the best book he had ever written. How are you? Do let me know. Strange to say, I am always pretty well. It makes a lot of difference to know I must not fall ill here under any circumstances. I always find sufficient strength for concentrated reading, but not always for writing, though from time to time I can manage that quite well too. How I shall get used to living in company again I don't know.

February 1st 1944

Carpe diem—which for me means that I seize every chance of sending you my best wishes. In the first place, I could write for a whole week without finishing everything I've got to tell you, and secondly one never knows how much longer it's likely to last. . . .

I daresay you have heard about the bad nights we have had just lately, especially on Jan. 30th. Those bombed out the previous night came to me next morning for a little comfort. I am afraid however I make a bad comforter: I can listen all right, but hardly ever find anything to say. But perhaps the way one asks about some things and is silent about others helps to suggest what really matters. But I am severe with

[98

some wrong-headed endeavours to explain away distress, for so far from being a comfort they are the exact opposite. And it does seem to me more important that we should really experience certain kinds of distress, rather than try to bottle it up or explain it away. I make no attempt to explain it, and I'm sure that is the right way to begin, though it is only a beginning, and I seldom seem to get beyond it. I am often inclined to think that real comfort must break in just as unexpectedly as the distress. But I grant you that may be a subterfuge.

Something which puzzles me and seems to puzzle many others as well is, how quickly we forget about a night's bombing. Even a few minutes after the all clear, everything we were thinking about while the raid was on seems to vanish into thin air. With Luther a flash of lightning was enough to alter the whole course of his life for years to come. What has happened to this kind of memory to-day? Does it not explain why we sit so lightly to the ties of love and marriage, of friendship and loyalty? Nothing holds us, nothing is firm. Everything is here to-day and gone to-morrow. Goodness, beauty and truth, however, and all great accomplishments need time, permanence and memory, or else they deteriorate. The man who has no urge to do his duty to the past and to shape the future is a man without a memory, and there seems to me no way of getting hold of such a person and bringing him to his senses. Every word, even if it impresses him for a moment, goes through one ear and out of the other. What is to be done about him? It is a tremendous pastoral problem, this. You put it very well in a recent letter of yours: people feel at home so quickly and so shamelessly! I am going to pinch that sentence from you and make use of it myself! . . .

By the way have you noticed how difficult it is for the uneducated to make up their minds about things, and how they let themselves be influenced by the most trifling considerations? I think it is most extraordinary. The difference between thinking about things and about persons is something that has to be learnt, and many never learn it. . . .

February 2nd 1944

Am I right in thinking you are stationed north of Rome? I do hope you will get a chance of having another look at the city. It must be tantalizing to be hanging about just in front of the gates, and not to be allowed to go in. There is little comfort in knowing you have seen it already.

How much longer I must continue amusing myself in my present abode is no more certain now than it was eight weeks ago. I am using every day to do as much reading and work as possible, for what will happen afterwards is anybody's guess. Unfortunately I am handicapped by the difficulty in getting hold of books, which upsets all my plans. My real ambition was to become thoroughly familiar with the nineteenth century in Germany. The biggest gap up to now is a working knowledge of Dilthey, but it does not seem to be possible to get hold of his books. And then there is another gap in my knowledge which is most painful, and that's natural science, though there's nothing to be done about it at this stage, I'm afraid.

My present companion whom I have mentioned several times in my letters is getting worse and worse. He has two colleagues here, one of whom spends the whole day moaning and groaning, and the other literally messes his trousers every time the alarm goes, and last night even when the alert was sounded! When he whined about it to me yesterday I burst out laughing and gave him a piece of my mind. He then tried to tell me how wrong it was to make light of somebody else's sufferings and to condemn him. That was really too much for me, and I told him in no uncertain terms what I thought of people who can be very hard on others and make grand speeches about living dangerously, etc., etc., and then crumple up themselves under the slightest test of endurance. It was downright disgraceful, I said, and I had no sympathy whatever with such behaviour. And I would have specimens like that thrown out of the party for making such fools of themselves. He was flabbergasted, and I daresay he thinks I'm a pretty doubtful sort of Christian after all that. Anyhow, his behaviour

[100

is becoming almost a byword here, and he can't like that very much. I find it all very instructive, though it's one of the most disgusting cases I've come across so far. I don't believe I find it easy to despise anyone in real trouble, and I have made that perfectly clear, which no doubt made his hair stand on end; but I can only regard that as contemptible. There are lads here of 17 or 18 in much more dangerous places during the raids, whose behaviour is irreproachable, while these . . . I had almost used a military expression which would have astounded you—go around whining. Really, it makes me sick. We all have our weak spots, I suppose.

I hope you won't think I have been too hard on him. But there's a kind of weakness Christianity will not stand for, but which everyone seems to expect Christianity to tolerate. We must take care that the contours don't get blurred.

Yesterday S. brought me the big volume on Magdeburg Cathedral. I am quite thrilled with the sculptures, especially some of the wise virgins. The bliss on these very earthly, almost peasant-like faces is a joy to behold. You will of course know them well.

February 12th 1944

I was in bed for a few days with a touch of the 'flu, but I am up again, thank goodness. For I daresay I shall need all my wits about me for the next week or two. Meanwhile I shall get as much reading and writing done as I can. Heaven knows when I shall have another chance.

Are you already enjoying a taste of spring? Here winter is only just beginning. In my dreams I live a good deal in nature, in the woods and meadows of Friedrichsbrunn or on the slopes—the slopes from which one can look beyond Treseburg to the Brocken.—I lie on my back and watch the clouds sailing past on the breeze and listen to the murmur of the wood. What a profound effect such memories of childhood have on the human character. I cannot imagine myself ever having lived up in the mountains or by the sea; it just does not fit my nature. It is the hills of central Germany, the Harz Mountains, the Thuringian forest, the Weserberge, which belong to me and have made me what I am. Of course there is a commonplace Harz and a hikers' Weserberge, just as there is a mundane and a Nietzschian Engadine, a romantic Rhineland, a Berliner's Baltic and a pretty-pretty fisherman's poverty and melancholy. So perhaps my midland hills are bourgeois, in the sense of what is natural, not too high, modest and self-satisfied, non-ideological, content with concrete realities, and above all not given to self-advertisement. It would be very tempting to pursue this sociological treatment of nature further some day. By the way, I can see now what Stifter means by distinguishing simpleness (*Einfalt*) and simplicity (*Einfachheit*). Stifter displays not simpleness but simplicity, just as the bourgeois is marked by simplicity. Simpleness is an æsthetic category, even in theology. Was not Winkelmann right when he spoke of the noble simpleness of classical art? Though that certainly does not apply to the Laocoon, 'Still greatness' I find very good. Simplicity is an ethical category. Simplicity is a quality which can be acquired, simpleness is innate. Simplicity may be acquired by education and may be cultivated, and indeed it is one of the essential objects of education and culture. Simpleness is a gift. The two things are related, it seems to me, much as purity and moderation. One can only be pure in relation to one's origin or goal, i.e. in relation to baptism or to forgiveness in the Eucharist. Like simpleness it is a category which denotes integrity. Once we have lost that purity—and we have all lost it—it can only be granted again in faith. But in ourselves, as living and growing persons, we can no longer be pure, but only moderate, and that is a proper and necessary object of education and culture.

What do you think of the Italian landscape? Is there any Italian school of landscape painters, anything comparable to Thoma, or even Claude Lorrain, Ruysdael or Turner? Or is nature there so completely absorbed into art that it cannot be looked at for its own sake? All the good pictures I can think of are of city life; there seems to be nothing in the way of pure landscape.

[102

February 13th 1944

I often notice here, both in myself and in others, the difference between the urge to pass on gossip, the desire for conversation and the need of confession. The urge to retail gossip is no doubt very attractive in women, but I find it repugnant in men. Everybody here seems to gossip indiscriminately about his private affairs, no matter whether others show any interest or not, merely for the sake of hearing themselves speak. It is an almost physical urge, but if you manage to suppress it for a few hours, you are afterwards glad you did not let yourself go. It often fills me with shame here to see how readily men demean themselves just for a bit of gossip, how they prate incessantly about their own private affairs to people who don't deserve it, and who hardly even listen. And the strangest thing about it is that they have no regard whatever for truth; all they want to do is to talk about themselves, whether what they say is true or not. The desire for a good conversation is a very different matter; there is something genuinely intellectual about that. Unfortunately there are few people here who are capable of carrying on a conversation beyond the range of immediate personal concern. Very different again is the need for confession. That, I am convinced, is a rarity here. For in the first place people here aren't worried about sin, whether their own or anybody else's. I daresay you have noticed in the prayers for prisoners I sent you how I soft-pedalled prayer for forgiveness. I thought it would be a mistake, both pastorally, and because of hard facts, to be too rigid about it. We must talk about that some day.

February 14th 1944

It looks as if during the next week or so my fate will be decided one way or the other. I hope it will. If by any chance they should send me in Martin's[1] direction (though I don't much think they will) please don't get upset. I am not in the

[1] He means the concentration camp at Dachau, where Martin Niemöller was confined.

least bit worried, at any rate about my personal fate. So you mustn't worry either.

February 21st 1944

. . . I am sorry to have to tell you that it does not look as though I shall be out of here before Easter now.

. . . I am wondering whether my excessive scrupulousness, which you often used to shake your head about with amusement (I am thinking of our travels!) is not really the other side of bourgeois existence. I mean, is it not a part of our faithlessness which hides below the surface all the time we are secure, but comes to the top in times of insecurity in the form of 'dread' (I don't mean cowardice, which is something quite different: dread can be manifested in rash daring just as much as in cowardice), dread in the face of straightforward, simple duty, dread in having to make vital decisions. I have often wondered when it is that the moment comes for us to throw up the sponge and abandon our resistance to fate. Resistance and submission are both equally necessary at different times. Don Quixote is the symbol of resistance carried on to the point of folly, and similarly Michael Kohlhaas insisted on his rights until it became his own undoing. In both cases resistance in the end defeats its own object, and vanishes into illusion and fantasy. Sancho Panza is the type of complacent and sly accommodation to things as they are. I am sure we must rise to the great responsibilities which are peculiarly our own, and yet at the same time fulfil the commonplace tasks of daily life. We must sally forth to defy fate—I think the neuter gender of *Schicksal* (fate) is significant—with just as much resolution as we submit to it when the time comes. One can only speak of providence on the other side of this dialectical process. God encounters us not only as a Thou, but also disguised as an It; so in the last resort my question is how we are to find the Thou in this It (i.e. fate). In other words, how does fate become providence? It is impossible therefore to define the boundary between resistance and submission in the abstract. Faith demands this elasticity of behaviour. Only so

[104

can we stand our ground in each situation as it comes along, and turn it to gain.

February 23rd 1944

If you manage to get to Rome during Holy Week, do try and get to the service at St. Peter's on Maundy Thursday afternoon (it lasts roughly from two to six). It is really the service for Good Friday, since the Roman Church anticipates its feasts from noon on the day before. I seem to remember, though I am not quite certain, that there is also a big service on the Wednesday. On Maundy Thursday all the twelve candles on the altar are put out as a symbol of the flight of the disciples, until at last there is only one candle left burning in the middle (for Christ). After that comes the washing of the altar. Early on Easter Eve, shortly before 7 a.m. there is the blessing of the font (I have a vague memory that it is connected with the ordination of young priests). Then at 12 noon the great Easter Alleluia is sung, the organ peals forth again, the mass bells ring, and the pictures are unveiled. Strictly speaking this is the celebration of Easter. Somewhere in Rome I also saw a Greek Orthodox service, which impressed me very much —it's more than twenty years ago! The service on Easter Eve in the Lateran (it starts in the baptistry) is also very famous. If you happen to be on Monte Pincio towards sunset, do drop into the Church of Trinita del Monte, and see whether the nuns are singing just at that time. I once heard them, and was very much impressed. I believe it is even mentioned in Baedecker.

I wonder if you are directly concerned with the fighting where you are? I suppose it's mainly a question of air raids, as it is here. The increase of air activity during the last ten days or so, especially during daylight, rather suggests that the English are probing our air power as a prelude to invasion, and as a means of pinning down our forces inside Germany.

The longer we are uprooted from professional activities and our private lives, the more it brings home to us how fragmentary our lives are compared with those of our parents.

105]

The portraits of the great savants in Harnack's *History of the Academy* make me acutely aware of that, and almost reduce me to melancholy. What chance have any of us to-day of producing a real *magnum opus*? How can we do all the research, the assimilation and sorting out of material which such a thing entails? Where to-day is that combination of fine carefreeness and large-scale planning that goes with such a life? I am quite sure that technicians and scientists, the only people who are still free to work, have nothing of the kind to show to-day. The 'polymath' had already died out by the close of the eighteenth century, and in the following century intensive education replaced extensive, so that by the end of it the specialist had evolved. The consequence is that to-day everyone is a mere technician, even the artist (in music the ideal is good form, in painting and literature no more than extreme moderation). That means however that culture has become a torso. The important thing to-day however is that people should be able to discern from the fragment of our life how the whole was arranged and planned, and of what material it consists. For there are some fragments which are only worth throwing into the dustbin, and even a decent hell is far too good for them. But there are other fragments whose importance lasts for centuries, because their completion can only be a matter for God, and therefore they are fragments which must be fragments.—I am thinking for example of the art of the fugue. If our life is but the remotest reflection of such a fragment, if in a short time we accumulate a wealth of themes and weld them together into a pleasing harmony and keep the great counterpoint going all through, so that, when it comes to an untimely conclusion, we can at least still sing the choral, *Vor deinen Thron tret' ich allhier*—then let us not bemoan the fragmentariness of our life, but rather rejoice in it. I can never get away from Jeremiah 45. I wonder if you still remember that Saturday evening in Finkenwald when I expounded it? Here too is a necessary fragment of life—'but thy life I will give unto thee for a prey.' . . .

. . . I am glad to hear that you have found a tolerable companion, so different from what you usually get. If only I could be there instead! I wonder if we shall ever make it. Or shall we perhaps keep Easter here as in days of old? You see, I'm not giving up hope. And you must not, either.

March 1st 1944

What a wonderful day it will be when we can discuss all we have been through and learnt during a whole year. For myself at any rate this is one of the greatest hopes the immediate future holds. No doubt like me you find it hard to imagine that such a day will ever come. It is so hard to believe that there is any chance of our overcoming all the obstacles in our way, yet 'that which tarries is all the sweeter when it comes'. And I must say, I am entering upon this new month with great hopes, and I think you must be too. I am redoubling my efforts to make the best use of my last weeks here. No doubt you too are learning lessons which will be of inestimable value for you all through your life. To be daily and hourly in danger, which is something we are nearly all having to go through just now, is a wonderful help in teaching us to use the present moment, to 'buy up the time'. Sometimes I feel my life is lasting just so long as there is something for me to live and work for.

March 9th 1944

I have heard from you again to-day, and am glad to know that you are at least finding things tolerable. And although that is not much (for we expect life to be more than just tolerable), there's some comfort in that, so long as we look upon our present condition as a kind of 'intermediate state'. If only we knew how long this purgatory is likely to last! It seems now that *I* shall have to wait until May. Isn't this dawdling scandalous?

. . . Sepp[1] is home again. He has fought his way through with all his old resilience and defiance.

[1] Dr. Joseph Müller of Munich, who had been acquitted, and whom B. wrongly supposed to have been released.

I haven't yet answered your remarks about Michelangelo, Burckhardt and *hilaritas*. What you say about Burckhardt's theses is certainly illuminating, but surely *hilaritas* means not only cheerfulness, in the classical sense of the word, such as we find in Raphael and Mozart. What about Walter von der Vogelweide, the Knight of Bamberg, Luther, Lessing, Rubens, Hugo Wolf and Karl Barth, to mention only a few? Surely they also have a kind of *hilaritas*, which might be described as confidence in their own work, a certain boldness and defiance of the world and of popular opinion, a steadfast certainty that what they are doing will benefit the world, even though it does not approve, a magnificent self-assurance. I grant you, Michelangelo, Rembrandt, and at a considerable remove, Kierkegaard and Nietzsche, are in quite a different class from the ones I have mentioned. There is something less evident, less definitive and conclusive about their work, less conviction, detachment and humour. All the same, I should not refuse them the word *hilaritas* in the sense I have described, as a necessary attribute of greatness. Here lies the limitation of Burckhardt, a limitation of which he was conscious. I have recently been studying the secularist movement of the thirteenth century. It was stamped not by the Renaissance, but by the Middle Ages, and it arose no doubt from the struggle between the Empire and the Papacy. It comes out in Walther, in the Nibelungen, and in Parsifal.—What an astonishing tolerance Parsifal's half-brother Feirefiz shews to the Mohammedans!—in Naumburg and Magdeburg cathedrals. Its worldliness is not emancipated, but Christian, though anticlerical. When did this worldliness, so different as it is from the Renaissance variety, come to an end? A trace of it seems to survive in Lessing, as compared with western Enlightenment, and in a different way in Goethe, then later in Stifter and Mörike, to say nothing of Claudius and Gotthelf, but there is nothing of it to be found in Schiller and the idealists. It would be worth while drawing up a good genealogy here. But that raises the problem of the value of classical antiquity. Is it still a relevant problem and a source of inspiration for us or not? The modern treatment of it under the heading 'City-state man' is already out of date. The classical treatment of it from the æsthetic point of view has but a limited appeal to-day, and is somewhat of a museum piece. The fundamental values of humanism, humanity, tolerance, tenderness and moderation are already apparent in Wolfram von Eschenbach and in the Knight of Bamberg, where they are present in the loveliest form, and more accessible and relevant to us than in classical antiquity itself. Does the interpretation of history which prevailed from Ranke to Delbrück as a continuity consisting of classical antiquity, the middle ages and the modern world really hold good? Or was Spengler right with his theory of cultural phases as self-contained cycles? The belief in historical continuity really goes back to Hegel, who regards the historical process as culminating in the modern world, i.e. in his own philosophy. Thus despite Ranke's assertion that every moment of history is directly related to God (which might have supplied a corrective, though it failed to do so), the idea of history as a continuous development has its roots in idealism. Spengler's morphology is biological, and that is its particular limitation—what does he mean by the senescence and decline of a culture? It means, however, that we cannot accept the classics as the basis of education, as the idealists did, nor can we eliminate classical antiquity from our phase of civilization biologically and morphologically, like Spengler. Until further light has been thrown on the whole subject, the best thing to do is to base our attitude to the past solely on the facts and achievements of any given period, and not on some abstract philosophy of history. I am afraid I have always felt cool towards the Renaissance and classicism; they both seem so remote, and I cannot make them my own. I wonder whether knowledge of other countries and an intimate contact with them is not a more important element for education to-day than a knowledge of the classics? Of course, in both cases there is a danger of parochialism. Yet it is perhaps one of the most important things we have to do, to see that our contacts with other nations are not confined to politics and commerce, but are really productive of cultural enrichment. In this way we should be tapping an hitherto unused source for the

109]

fertilizing of our culture, and at the same time carrying on an old European tradition.

The wireless has just announced the approach of strong contingents of enemy aircraft. We saw quite a lot of the last two daylight raids on Berlin; we could see considerable formations flying through a cloudless sky and leaving behind them a trail of condensation. At times there was a considerable amount of ack-ack too. The alarm was on for two and a half hours yesterday, longer than any of the night raids. To-day the sky is overcast. . . . The siren is just going, so I must break off and write again later.—It lasted two hours. 'Bombs were dropped in all parts of the city', says the wireless. For two months here I have been trying to observe how far people still have any belief in transcendent reality. Three notions seems to be quite common. 1. People say 'Cross fingers', apparently attaching some sort of power to the accompanying thought. They don't want to feel alone in the hour of danger, and want to be sure of some invisible presence. 2. 'Touch wood' is the universal exclamation when the prospect of a raid the next night is being discussed. This seems to be a recollection of the wrath of God on the *hybris* of man, in other words a metaphysical, and not merely a moral ground for humility. 3. 'You can't run away from fate', and as a corollary, everyone ought to stay where he is put. On a Christian interpretation these three points might be regarded as a recollection of intercessory prayer and the Church, of the wrath and grace of God and of divine providence. To the last we might add another phrase frequently heard here: 'All these things are sent to try us.' There does not seem to be any trace of a recollection of eschatology. Perhaps you have observed something different where you are?

This is my second passiontide here. People sometimes suggest in their letters that I am suffering here. Personally, I shrink from such a thought, for it seems a profanation of that word. These things mustn't be dramatized. I should not be at all surprised if you, and indeed almost everyone else now-a-days, are suffering more than I am. Of course, there's a good deal here that's appalling, but isn't it the same everywhere? Perhaps we have tended to exaggerate the whole question of suffering,

[110

and have been too solemn about it. I have often wondered before now why it is that Catholics take such little notice of this sort of thing. Is it because they are stronger than we are? Perhaps they know from their own history better than we do what real suffering and martyrdom are, and therefore they pass over petty inconveniences and obstacles in silence. I believe for instance that all real suffering contains an element of physical pain. We are always too much inclined to emphasize the sufferings of the soul. Yet that is just what Christ is supposed to have removed from us, and I cannot find anything in the New Testament about it, or in the acts of the early martyrs. There is all the difference in the world between the Church's own sufferings and the untoward experiences of one of her servants. I am sure we need a good deal of correction on this point. Frankly speaking, I sometimes feel almost ashamed to think how much we have talked about our own sufferings. Indeed, real suffering must be quite a different matter and have a quite different dimension, from anything I have experienced hitherto. Enough for to-day. When shall we be able to talk together again? Take care of yourself, and make the most of the beautiful country you are in. Spread *hilaritas* around you, and mind you keep it yourself!

March 19th 1944

With the news of the heavy fighting in your neighbourhood you are hardly ever out of my thoughts. Every word I read in the Bible and the hymns I apply to you. You ... must be feeling very homesick during these dangerous days, and every letter will only make it worse. But surely, it is the mark of a grown-up man, as compared with a callow youth, that he finds his centre of gravity wherever he happens to be at the moment, and however much he longs for the object of his desire, it cannot prevent him from staying at his post and doing his duty? The adolescent is never quite 'all there': if he were, he wouldn't be an adolescent, but a dullard. There is a wholeness about the fully grown man which makes him concentrate on the present moment. He may have unsatisfied desires, but he always keeps them out of sight, and manages to master them some way or other. And the more need he has of self-mastery, the more confidence he will inspire among his comrades, especially the younger ones, who are still on the road he has already travelled. Clinging too much to our desires easily prevents us from being what we ought to be and can be. Desires repeatedly mastered for the sake of present duty make us, conversely, all the richer. To be without desire is a mark of poverty. At the moment I am surrounded by people who cling to their desires, so much so that they haven't any interest for others: they give up listening, and are incapable of loving their neighbour. I think we should live even in this place as though we had no desires and no future to hope for, and just be our true selves. It is remarkable what an influence one acquires in this way over other men. They come and confide in us, and let us speak to them. I am writing to you about this because I think there is a lot for you to do too just now, and later on you will be glad to think that you have done your best. When we know that a friend is in danger, we somehow want to be assured that he is being his true self. We can have a full life even when we haven't got everything we want—that is what I am really trying to say. Forgive me for troubling you with my thoughts, but thinking is my chief amusement here. I'm sure you'll understand. I ought to add, by the way, that I am more convinced than ever that it won't be long before *our* wishes are fulfilled, and there's no need for *us* to resign ourselves to the worst.

. . . I am going through another spell of finding it difficult to read the Bible. I never know quite what to make of it. I don't feel guilty at all about it, and I know it won't be long before I return to it again with renewed zest. Is it just a psychological process? I am almost inclined to think so. Do you remember how we often used to find it like that when we were together? True, there is always a danger of indolence, but it would be wrong to get fussed about it. Far better to trust that after wobbling a bit the compass will come to rest in the right direction. Don't you agree? . . . It's almost a year since we spent those last days working together. . . . I wish I knew

[112

what the future has in store for us. I wonder if we shall be together again, perhaps in some work—or must we be content with the past?

March 24th 1944

I daresay you are thinking a great deal about the baby's christening. My chief reason for writing is a feeling that you must be depressed by the apparent illogicality of it all. We often used to say that children ought to be baptized at the earliest possible moment, even when the father cannot be present. The reasons for this are clear enough. Yet I cannot but think you are right to wait. For though I still think an early baptism is a good thing, and very desirable (especially as an example to the parish, provided you do it with a sincere faith in the efficacy of the sacrament), there is something to be said for the father waiting until he can be present at the service and take part in the prayers for his child. And when I examine my own feelings on the subject, I must confess I am chiefly influenced by the consideration that God loves the unbaptized child who is intended for baptism. The New Testament lays down no law about infant baptism, and it is in fact a gift of grace which has been granted to the Church. Hence it can be a striking testimony of faith for the parish. But to force oneself to proceed with it without feeling the compulsion of faith is certainly not biblical. Regarded purely as a demonstration, infant baptism cannot be justified. God will undoubtedly hear our prayers for the child when we ask him to send the day soon when we can bring him to the font. So long as there is every prospect of this day coming soon, I cannot believe that God is particularly concerned about the exact date. Hence we can trust in a merciful providence and wait until we can do with sincerity what for the moment we should feel an oppressive burden. . . . So I should wait a little while without any scruples, in the hope that we shall see our way more clearly later. I am sure it will be better for the actual baptism: it will make the whole thing more sincere, which is a much more important consideration than the outward performance of the rite.

113]

. . . You are getting to know my favourite country far better than I know it myself. How I should love to sit with you in the car and see the Cecilia Metella or Hadrian's Villa. I have never been able to make much of the Pietà.[1] You must explain to me some time what it is you like about it so much.

March 25th 1944

We had a very lively time last night. The view from the roof here over the city was staggering. I still haven't heard anything about the rest of the family. My parents left for P. yesterday, thank God, but there wasn't much doing in the west. It is absurd how one can't help hoping when an air raid is announced, that it will be the turn of other places this time. The principle is the same as that of 'Holy St. Florian, spare my house, and set others on fire'. 'Perhaps they won't get any further than Magdeburg or Stettin this time'—how often have I heard that pious wish! Such moments bring home to one the corruption of human nature and the truth of original sin, and to that extent it is probably a salutary experience. Incidentally, there has been a noticeable increase in air activity during the last day or two, and it makes one wonder whether it is not meant as a makeshift substitute for the long heralded invasion.

I shall not be able to make any plans for the future until May. I am gradually losing faith in all these forecasts, and have ceased to take any notice of them. Quite likely they will be telling me then that it may be July. In any case, my own personal future is of secondary importance compared with the general situation, though the two things are very closely connected. So I hope we shall still have a chance of discussing our plans for the future. . . .

I am still all right here. Somehow I seem to have become part of the furniture, and I get less peace and quietness than I should like. You are quite right about the rarity of landscape painting in Southern Europe. Is the south of France an exception? What about Claude Lorrain? Yet it seems to flourish in Germany and England. I suppose the southerner has the

[1] By Michelangelo, in St. Peter's.

[114

beauties of nature to enjoy, while for us they are so rare that they induce a wistful longing for them. By the way, to change the subject, Mörike once said that 'where beauty is, there is happiness as well'. Does that not fit in with Burckhardt? It is all too easy for us to acquiesce in Nietzsche's crude alternatives of 'Apolline' and 'Dionysian', or as we should say to-day, demonic beauty. Nothing could be further from the truth. Take for example Brueghel or Velasquez, or Hans Thoma, Leopold von Kalkreuth, or the French impressionists. Here we have a beauty which is neither classical nor demonic, but is simply earthly, though it has its own proper place. For my part, I must confess this is the only kind of beauty that appeals to me. I would also add the Magdeburg virgins I mentioned the other day. This rather suggests that the Faustian interpretation of Gothic art is altogether on the wrong lines. How else can we explain the remarkable contrast between the plastic arts and architecture? . . .

Must close for to-day, otherwise you'll never get through this letter. I am so glad to think of how you played *Lobe den Herrn* that time. It did us all a lot of good!

March 27th 1944

Perhaps I ought to send you my good wishes for Easter already, for I have no notion how long my letters take to reach you. In looking through *Das Neue Lied* during these days, I am constantly reminded how it is to you principally that I owe my enjoyment of the Easter hymns. It's a year now since I actually heard a hymn. But the music of the inward ear can often surpass that which we hear physically, so long as we really concentrate. Isn't that remarkable? Indeed, there is something purer about it, and in a way music acquires thereby a 'new body'! There are only a few pieces I know well enough to be able always to hear them inwardly, but I get on particularly well with the Easter hymns. My appreciation of the music Beethoven composed after he went deaf has become more 'existential', and in particular, the great variation from Opus III:

By the way, I heard the Sunday concert from 6-7 p.m. the other day, though it was on an atrocious wireless set.

Speaking of Easter, do we not attach more importance nowadays to the act of dying than to death itself? We are much more concerned with getting over the act of dying than with being victorious over death. Socrates mastered the art of dying; Christ overcame death as the ἔσχατος ἐχθρος, the last enemy (1 Corinthians 15.27). There is a real difference between the two things. The one is within human capacity, the other implies resurrection. We need not *ars moriendi*, the art of dying, but the resurrection of Christ to invigorate and cleanse the world to-day. Here is the answer to δὸς μοί ποῦ στῶ καὶ κινήσω τὴν γῆν, give me where I stand and I will move the earth. What a tremendous difference it would make if a few people really believed and acted upon that. To live in the light of the resurrection—that is the meaning of Easter. Do you not also find that so few people seem to know what light it is they live by? This *perturbatio animorum* is exceedingly common. It is an unconscious waiting for the word of deliverance, though the time is hardly ripe yet for it to be heard. But the time will come, and perhaps this Easter is one of the last chances we shall have to prepare ourselves for our future task. I hope you will be able to enjoy it despite all the hardships you are having to bear. Good-bye, I must close now.

April 2nd 1944

Now that Easter will apparently come and go without our being at home and meeting again, I am putting off hope until Whitsun at the latest. What do you think about it? You must be having a glorious spring. Just imagine, I have taken up graphology again, and am just working through Ludwig Klages' book. I'm not going to try it out on my friends and relations. There are others here who seem to be interested in it too. I am convinced there is something in it. No doubt you remember how successful I was at it in my student days, so much so that it became embarrassing, and I gave it up. But I think I have got over the dangers of psychology by now, and I am very interested in it again. I wish I could discuss it with you. If it gets uncanny again, I shall drop it at once. There are two requirements, sensitivity and an acute power of observation, the second of which you possess to a much greater degree than I. If you like I will write you further on the subject.

In Karl Kindt's 800-page biography of Klopstock I found some very striking extracts from the latter's play, *Der Tod Adams*, which is about the death of the first man. The ode is interesting enough, and the actual play is just terrific. I had often thought of trying to rehabilitate Klopstock, so I find the book very interesting.

I have here quite a detailed map of the environs of Rome, and I often look at it when thinking of you, and imagine you going round the streets, so familiar to you from long acquaintance, hearing the sounds of war not so very far away, and surveying the Mediterranean from the mountains. . . .

April 11th 1944

I really wanted to write to you over the Easter season, but I had so many well-meaning visitors that I had less peace and quiet than I could have desired. . . . I have become so inured to quietness and solitude that after a short time I long for it again. I cannot imagine myself spending the day as I used to with you, or as you do now. . . . I certainly would like to have a good talk with someone, but senseless gossip gets on my nerves terribly.

I wonder how you have been spending Easter. Were you in Rome? And have you got over your homesickness? I can well imagine you find it harder than I do. For it cannot be got over without diversion and distraction. It takes a terrific amount of effort and one needs a good deal of time to oneself. I find these first warm days of spring rather trying, and no doubt you do too. Nature is rediscovering herself, but the tensions in our

117]

own lives and in the society we live in are just as bad as before, and the discord between them is particularly acute. Or perhaps it is just homesickness, and it is good for us to feel it acutely again. As far as my own life is concerned, I must say I have plenty to aim at, to do and to hope for to keep me fully absorbed, yet without wanting anything for myself. And perhaps that has made me old before my time. It has made everything so prosaic and matter of fact. How few there are who can still indulge some strong personal feeling, who make a real effort and spend all their strength in enduring their longing, assimilating it and turning it to gain in their lives! Those sentimental radio 'hits' with their artificial naïveté and their barren crudities are the lamentable remains and the maximum of what people will tolerate in the way of spiritual effort. It is a sad desolation and impoverishment. Let us by contrast rejoice when something affects us deeply, and regard the accompanying pains as an enrichment of soul. High tensions produce big sparks—is that not a physical fact? If I'm wrong translate it into the appropriate jargon. I have long had a special affection for the season between Easter and Ascension Day. Here is another great tension. How can men endure earthly tensions if they know nothing of the tension between earth and heaven? Have you by any chance got a copy of *Das Neue Lied* with you? I have vivid memories of learning the Ascensiontide hymns with you, especially *Auf diesen Tag bedenken wir*, which is still one of my favourites. By the way, to-day we are entering on the tenth year of our friendship, a large slice in a man's life. And we have shared everything as intensely during the last year as we did during the former years when we were together.

. . . I can't help feeling that when we do get home again, it will be together. I have been told I ought not to look for any change in my position in the immediate future—and that after all the promises they made every fortnight. I don't think it's either right or clever of them, and I have my own ideas on the subject, which I should very much like to tell you of. But as I can't get my own way, I must just make the best of it, and continue to hope for Whitsun.

Yesterday I heard someone say he felt that the last years had been completely wasted as far as he was concerned. I have never felt like that, not even for a moment. Nor have I ever regretted my decision in the summer of 1939,[1] and strange as it may seem, I am convinced that my life has followed a straight and even course, at any rate so far as its outward circumstances are concerned. It has been an uninterrupted enrichment of my experience, for which I can only be thankful. If I should end my days here like this, that would have a meaning I could understand. On the other hand my time here may be a thorough preparation for a fresh start, for a new job of work when peace comes again. . . . I will close now for to-day, for I have another graphological analysis to do. That's how I while away the time when I cannot do any serious work. I'm afraid this letter is a bit disjointed owing to repeated interruptions while I was writing it.

April 22nd 1944

You say my time here will be very important for my work, and that you're looking forward to what I shall have to tell you later, and to read what I have produced so far.— Well, you mustn't expect too much: I have certainly learnt a great deal, but I don't think I have changed very much. There are some who change a lot, but many hardly change at all. I don't believe I have ever changed very much, except at two periods in my life, the first under the first conscious impact of Papa's personality, and the second when I was abroad. I think you are very much the same. Self-development is of course an entirely different matter. Neither of us has had any sudden break in our lives. Of course we have deliberately broken with a great deal, but that again is an entirely different matter. Our present experiences hardly represent a real break in the passive sense. In the old days I often used to long for such a break, but I think quite differently about it to-day. Continuity with our past is a wonderful gift. St. Paul wrote II Timothy 1.3a as well as I Timothy 1.13! I often marvel how little I worry over

[1] To return from the U.S.A. to Germany.

past mistakes compared with most of the others here. It never occurs to me how different everything would be to-day if only I had acted differently in the past. I can't help feeling that everything has taken its natural course; it has all been inevitable, straightforward, directed by a higher providence. Don't you feel the same?

Just lately I have been wondering why we grow insensitive to hardships in course of time. When I think how I felt a year ago it strikes me very much. To put it down to nature's self-protection isn't the whole story. There's more to it than that. We come to a clearer and more sober estimate of our own limitations and responsibilities, and that makes it possible for us genuinely to love our neighbours. So long as we are suffering from an exaggerated sense of our own importance we can never really love our neighbours: love of one's neighbour remains something vague and abstract. To-day I am able to take a calmer view of other people, of their needs and requirements, and so I am able to help them more. I would prefer to speak of illumination rather than insensitiveness. But of course it is always up to us to change the one into the other. On the other hand, I am sure we ought not to reproach ourselves because our feelings grow cooler and calmer in the course of time, though we must always be alive to the danger of becoming blind to everything, and even when we have reached the stage of illumination we must still keep a warm heart. Will these reflections be of any use to you?

I wonder what makes some days seem more oppressive than others. Is it just a matter of growing pains, or is it spiritual trial? Once they are over the world looks quite a different place again.

The other day I heard the angel scene from Palestrina on the wireless. It reminded me of Munich. Even then that was the only part that really impressed me. There's a great Palestrina fan here who was perplexed at my lack of enthusiasm for him, and was quite thrilled when I said how I enjoyed the angel scene.

For a long time I haven't been able to get down to any serious work, but now with the approach of spring I'm feeling

[120

more in the mood for it again. I hope to say something about what I'm doing next time. Meanwhile take care of yourself and keep your end up. I hope that in spite of everything we shall be able to meet again soon. What a joy that will be!

April 30th 1944

Another month gone! Do you find time flies as I do here? It often amazes me—and when will the month come when we shall meet again? Such tremendous events are taking place in the world outside, events which will have a profound effect on the course of our lives. This makes me wish I could write to you more frequently, if partly because I don't know how much longer I shall be able to, but above all because I want to make the most of what opportunities I have of sharing everything with you. I am firmly convinced that by the time you get this letter great decisions will have been reached on all fronts. During the coming weeks we shall have to be very brave: we must keep our wits about us and be prepared for the worst. I am reminded of the biblical δεῖ, and I feel as curious as the angels in I Peter 1.12 as to how God intends to resolve these apparently insoluble issues. I am sure God is about to do something which we can only accept with wonder and amazement. We shall, if we have eyes to see, realize the truth of Psalm 58.12b and Psalm 9.20f. And we shall have to repeat Jeremiah 45.5 to ourselves every day. It is harder for you to go through all this alone than it is for me, so I will think of you especially, as indeed I am already doing now.

How good it would be if we could go through this time together, standing side by side. But it is probably best for us to face it alone. I am so sorry I can't help you at all, except by thinking of you as I read the Bible every morning and evening, and often during the day. You really must not worry about me, for I'm getting on uncommonly well, and you would be astonished if you came to see me. They keep on telling me that I am 'radiating so much peace around me', and that I am 'ever so cheerful'. Very flattering, no doubt, but I'm afraid I don't always feel like that myself. You would be surprised and perhaps disturbed if you knew how my ideas on theology are taking shape. This is where I miss you most of all, for there is no one else who could help me so much to clarify my own mind. The thing that keeps coming back to me is, what *is* Christianity, and indeed what *is* Christ, for us to-day? The time when men could be told everything by means of words, whether theological or simply pious, is over, and so is the time of inwardness and conscience, which is to say the time of religion as such. We are proceeding towards a time of no religion at all: men as they are now simply cannot be religious any more. Even those who honestly describe themselves as 'religious' do not in the least act up to it, and so when they say 'religious' they evidently mean something quite different. Our whole nineteen-hundred-year-old Christian preaching and theology rests upon the 'religious premise' of man. What we call Christianity has always been a pattern—perhaps a true pattern—of religion. But if one day it becomes apparent that this *a priori* 'premise' simply does not exist, but was an historical and temporary form of human self-expression, i.e. if we reach the stage of being radically without religion—and I think this is more or less the case already, else how is it, for instance, that this war, unlike any of those before it, is not calling forth any 'religious' reaction?—what does that mean for 'Christianity'?

It means that the linchpin is removed from the whole structure of our Christianity to date, and the only people left for us to light on in the way of 'religion' are a few 'last survivals of the age of chivalry', or else one or two who are intellectually dishonest. Would they be the chosen few? Is it on this dubious group and none other that we are to pounce, in fervour, pique, or indignation, in order to sell them the goods we have to offer? Are we to fall upon one or two unhappy people in their weakest moment and force upon them a sort of religious coercion?

If we do not want to do this, if we had finally to put down the western pattern of Christianity as a mere preliminary stage to doing without religion altogether, what situation would result for us, for the Church? How can Christ become the

Lord even of those with no religion? If religion is no more than the garment of Christianity—and even that garment has had very different aspects at different periods—then what is a religionless Christianity? Barth, who is the only one to have started on this line of thought, has still not proceeded to its logical conclusion, but has arrived at a positivism of revelation which has nevertheless remained essentially a restoration. For the religionless working man, or indeed, man generally, nothing that makes any real difference is gained by that. The questions needing answers would surely be: What is the significance of a Church (church, parish, preaching, Christian life) in a religionless world? How do we speak of God without religion, i.e. without the temporally-influenced presuppositions of metaphysics, inwardness, and so on? How do we speak (but perhaps we are no longer capable of speaking of such things as we used to) in secular fashion of God? In what way are we in a religionless and secular sense Christians, in what way are we the *Ekklesia*, 'those who are called forth', not conceiving of ourselves religiously as specially favoured, but as wholly belonging to the world? Then Christ is no longer an object of religion, but something quite different, indeed and in truth the Lord of the world. Yet what does that signify? What is the place of worship and prayer in an entire absence of religion? Does the secret discipline, or, as the case may be, the distinction (which you have met with me before) between penultimate and ultimate, at this point acquire fresh importance? I must break off for to-day, so that the letter can be posted straight away. In two days I will write to you further on the subject. I hope you have a rough idea what I'm getting at, and that it does not bore you. Good-bye for the present. It isn't easy to keep writing without any echo from you. You must excuse me if that makes it rather a monologue!

I find after all I can carry on writing.—The Pauline question whether circumcision is a condition of justification is to-day, I consider, the question whether religion is a condition of salvation. Freedom from circumcision is at the same time freedom from religion. I often ask myself why a Christian instinct frequently draws me more to the religionless than to the religious, by which I mean not with any intention of evangelizing them, but rather, I might almost say, in 'brother-hood'. While I often shrink with religious people from speaking of God by name—because that Name somehow seems to me here not to ring true, and I strike myself as rather dishonest (it is especially bad when others start talking in religious jargon: then I dry up completely and feel somehow oppressed and ill at ease)—with people who have no religion I am able on occasion to speak of God quite openly and as it were natur-ally. Religious people speak of God when human perception is (often just from laziness) at an end, or human resources fail: it is really always the *Deus ex machina* they call to their aid, either for the so-called solving of insoluble problems or as support in human failure—always, that is to say, helping out human weakness or on the borders of human existence. Of necessity, that can only go on until men can, by their own strength, push those borders a little further, so that God becomes super-fluous as a *Deus ex machina*. I have come to be doubtful even about talking of 'borders of human existence'. Is even death to-day, since men are scarcely afraid of it any more, and sin, which they scarcely understand any more, still a genuine borderline? It always seems to me that in talking thus we are only seeking frantically to make room for God. I should like to speak of God not on the borders of life but at its centre, not in weakness but in strength, not, therefore, in man's suffering and death but in his life and prosperity. On the borders it seems to me better to hold our peace and leave the problem unsolved. Belief in the Resurrection is not the solution of the problem of death. The 'beyond' of God is not the beyond of our perceptive faculties. The transcendence of theory based on perception has nothing to do with the transcendence of God. God is the 'beyond' in the midst of our life. The Church stands not where human powers give out, on the borders, but in the centre of the village. That is the way it is in the Old Testament, and in this sense we still read the New Testament far too little on the basis of the Old. The outward aspect of this religionless Christianity, the form it takes, is something to which I am giving much thought, and I shall be writing to

[124

you about it again soon. It may be that on us in particular, midway between East and West, there will fall an important responsibility.

It would be grand to have a line from you on all this; indeed it would mean more to me than you can imagine, I'm sure. I suggest you should look at Proverbs 22.11, 12. There's something that will bar the way against any kind of pious escapism.

May 5th 1944

I imagine you must be on leave by now, and this letter will have to be sent on to you. Unfortunately that will mean it will be out of date by the time it reaches you, for life is so uncertain nowadays. Yet long experience suggests that everything remains as it is rather than suddenly changes, so I should like to write to you all the same. I'm getting along pretty well, and so is the case, though the date still hasn't been fixed. But all good things take us by surprise when they do come, so I'm waiting confidently for that.

A bit more about 'religionlessness'. I expect you remember Bultmann's paper on the demythologizing of the New Testament? My view of it to-day would be not that he went too far, as most people seem to think, but that he did not go far enough. It is not only the mythological conceptions, such as the miracles, the ascension and the like (which are not in principle separable from the conceptions of God, faith and so on) that are problematic, but the 'religious' conceptions themselves. You cannot, as Bultmann imagines, separate God and miracles, but you do have to be able to interpret and proclaim *both* of them in a 'non-religious' sense. Bultmann's approach is really at bottom the liberal one (i.e. abridging the Gospel), whereas I seek to think theologically.

What do I mean by 'interpret in a religious sense'? In my view, that means to speak on the one hand metaphysically, and on the other individualistically. Neither of these is relevant to the Bible message or to the man of to-day. Is it not true to say that individualistic concern for personal salvation has almost completely left us all? Are we not really under the

125]

impression that there are more important things than bothering about such a matter? (Perhaps not more important than the matter itself, but more than bothering about it.) I know it sounds pretty monstrous to say that. But is it not, at bottom, even Biblical? Is there any concern in the Old Testament about saving one's soul at all? Is not righteousness and the kingdom of God on earth the focus of everything, and is not Romans 3.14ff., too, the culmination of the view that in God alone is righteousness, and not in an individualistic doctrine of salvation? It is not with the next world that we are concerned, but with this world as created and preserved and set subject to laws and atoned for and made new. What is above the world is, in the Gospel, intended to exist *for* this world—I mean that not in the anthropocentric sense of liberal, pietistic, ethical theology, but in the Bible sense of the creation and of the incarnation, crucifixion, and resurrection of Jesus Christ.

Barth was the first theologian to begin the criticism of religion,—and that remains his really great merit—but he set in its place the positivist doctrine of revelation which says in effect, 'Take it or leave it': Virgin Birth, Trinity or anything else, everything which is an equally significant and necessary part of the whole, which latter has to be swallowed as a whole or not at all. That is not in accordance with the Bible. There are degrees of perception and degrees of significance, i.e. a secret discipline must be re-established whereby the *mysteries* of the Christian faith are preserved from profanation. The positivist doctrine of revelation makes it too easy for itself, setting up, as in the ultimate analysis it does, a law of faith, and mutilating what is, by the incarnation of Christ, a gift for us. The place of religion is taken by the Church—that is, in itself, as the Bible teaches it should be—but the world is made to depend upon itself and left to its own devices, and that is all wrong.

I am thinking over the problem at present how we may reinterpret in the manner 'of the world'—in the sense of the Old Testament and of John 1.14—the concepts of repentance, faith, justification, rebirth, sanctification and so on. I shall be writing to you again about that.

Forgive me for writing all this in German script—normally I only use it when making notes for myself. And perhaps my reason for writing all this is to clear my own mind, rather than for your edification. I don't really want to bother you with such problems, for I don't suppose you will find time to come to grips with them, and there's no need to worry you unnecessarily. But I can't help sharing my thoughts with you, for the simple reason that that's the only way I can clarify my own mind. If this doesn't suit you, please say so.—To-morrow is Cantate [the Fourth Sunday after Easter], and I shall be thinking of you, and enjoying pleasant memories. Good-bye. Be patient like me, and take care of yourself.

May 6th 1944

. . . I shall be writing about Christian 'egoism' next time —selfless self-love. I think we agree about that. Too much altruism is a bore, and makes too many claims. There is a kind of egoism which can be more selfless, and make less claims upon us.

Cantate

I have just heard some good music this morning by Reger and Hugo Distler, a good beginning for Sunday. The only jarring note was an interruption announcing that 'Enemy detachments were proceeding towards so and so'—the connexion between the two wasn't immediately obvious.

Last night I was thinking about the uses of mothers-in-law. I am sure they ought not to try and teach, for I can't see they have any right to do that. Their privilege is rather to have acquired a grown-up son or daughter, and they must regard that as an enrichment to their family, not as an opportunity to criticize. They may find their joy in their children, and give any help or advice they are asked for, but the marriage completely relieves them of any responsibility as teachers. That is really a privilege. I believe that a mother-in-law ought to be

127]

glad to see that someone else loves her child, and therefore she ought to put all other considerations into the background, especially any urge to mould character!

How few people seem to have a proper appreciation of reticence! The siren is just going, so more later. . . . It was pretty heavy again.

With regard to reticence, it all depends on *what* we are keeping to ourselves, and that we have *one* friend with whom we can share everything. . . . I think it is going too far to speak of the jealousy of mothers-in-law. It would be truer to say that there are two kinds of love, a mother's and a wife's, and this is the source of a great deal of misunderstanding. Yet, incidentally, it is much easier for the husband to get on with his mother-in-law than it is for the wife with hers, though the Bible gives a unique example of the contrary in Naomi and Ruth.

Just lately I've been taken once or twice into the city for judicial examination. The result has been most satisfactory. But as they still haven't fixed anything as regards the date, I'm really losing interest in my case. Often I don't think anything about it for weeks on end. Finis! May God take care of us all.

May 9th 1944

I am so glad to hear you are hoping to come home on leave soon. If you find you can manage to have the christening in a few days time, don't let the thought of my absence do anything to spoil your joy. I hope to try and write something special for the occasion, and you know I shall be with you in spirit. It is certainly painful to think that contrary to all expectation I shall not be with you on that day, but I have reconciled myself to it. I'm sure everything that happens to me has a purpose, even if it cuts right across our own wishes. As I see it, I am here for some purpose, and I only hope I'm living up to it. In the light of our supreme purpose all our personal privations and disappointments are trivial. It would be unworthy and wrongheaded to bemoan my present misfortunes on one of these rare occasions of joy like the

present. That would go entirely against the grain, and under-
mine my optimism with regard to my case. Grateful as we are
for every bit of private happiness that comes our way, we
must not for a moment lose sight of the great causes we are
living for, and they must cast light rather than gloom upon
your joy. I couldn't bear to think that I should be the cause of
spoiling your few weeks of happiness, after you have had to
fight so hard to get them. *That* would be a calamity, the other
is not. I am quite happy so long as I can help you to keep the
lustre of these spring days untarnished. Please don't think for
a moment that I am any loss to your company—far from it.
And above all don't think I find it an effort to write these
words; they represent my earnest entreaty, and your compli-
ance with them would only make me happy. If we did manage
to meet while you are on leave, I should be only too happy,
but don't put yourself out about it—I still have vivid memories of the 23rd December!—and please don't lose a single
day for the sake of spending a little time with me here. I know
you would be only too willing, but I should be terribly dis-
tressed if you did. But if your father did manage to arrange a
visit as he did last December, I should of course be most
grateful. Incidentally, I know we shall be both thinking of
each other as we read the text for to-morrow, and I'm very
glad you will both be able to read the Bible together again,
for it will be a great help to you not only while you are
together, but also later when you are separated again. Don't
let the shortness of your time together and the thought that
you must soon part overshadow the happiness of your leave.
Don't try and do too much. Let other people come and see
you and don't go round to see everyone yourselves. I shouldn't
be at all surprised if the next weeks bring important and
unexpected decisions which will have a profound effect on our
lives, yet I do hope you will get a few days of undisturbed
peace and quietness together. What a good thing you have
this opportunity of making your plans for the future together.

I should have loved to perform the baptism myself, but that's
neither here nor there. Above all, I hope the christening will
help you to realize that all your lives, the child's and your own,

are under the protection of God, and that you can look forward to the future with confidence. Are you going to choose the text for the baptism yourself? If so, what about II Timothy 2.1 or Proverbs 23.26 or 4.18 (I only came across the last one the other day; I think it's beautiful).

I don't want to bother you with too long a letter right at the beginning of your reunion. All I wanted to do was to send you my best wishes and tell you I'm sharing your joy. Mind you have plenty of good music!

May 16th 1944

I have just heard you have sent a message saying you hope to arrive this morning. You can't imagine how glad and relieved I am to think you can be here just now. For once I could almost say it's providential, a real answer to prayer, and maybe you will agree. I am still hoping to write something for the christening. What about Psalm 90.14 as a text? I might have suggested Isaiah 8.18, but it's rather too general.

May 18th 1944

I wanted to write something for the day of the baptism, and my chief reason for sending it is to show you that I'm thinking of you. . . . I hope this day will be a long-cherished memory, and that it will set the tone for your leave. That I'm afraid will be all too brief, but I hope you'll soon be home for good. Some memories are painful, others can be an inspiration: may the memory of this day be an inspiration to you when you are parted again. . . . Please don't harbour any regrets about me. Martin [Niemöller] has had nearly seven years of it—and that's very different. . . . I have just heard you are coming to see me to-morrow. How wonderful; I had given up all hope of it myself. So I'm spending this day getting ready for your visit. Who managed to arrange it? Whoever it was, I am most grateful.

May 19th 1944

I cannot tell you how much joy your visit has given me,

[130

and also your courage in coming, just the two of you together. It was marvellous. I was deeply moved to hear about your recent experiences. I'm in too great a hurry to go into detail to-day. Above all, I pray you may find that peace which you so badly need, both within and without, after all these upsets you've had lately. I was awfully sorry the alarm was on just when you came, and I breathed a sigh of relief when the commandant brought your telephone message. The meaning of things is often obscure. But don't you find it a relief to know that some things are unavoidable, and have just got to be endured, even though we can't see the purpose behind it all? That's something I have learnt more clearly here.

May 20th 1944 ✓

There is always a danger of intense love destroying what I might call the 'polyphony' of life. What I mean is that God requires that we should love him eternally with our whole hearts, yet not so as to compromise or diminish our earthly affections, but as a kind of *cantus firmus* to which the other melodies of life provide the counterpoint. Earthly affection is one of these contrapuntal themes, a theme which enjoys an autonomy of its own. Even the Bible can find room for the Song of Songs, and one could hardly have a more passionate and sensual love than is there portrayed (see 7.6). It is a good thing that that book is included in the Bible as a protest against those who believe that Christianity stands for the restraint of passion (is there any example of such restraint anywhere in the Old Testament?). Where the ground bass is firm and clear, there is nothing to stop the counterpoint from being developed to the utmost of its limits. Both ground bass and counterpoint are 'without confusion and yet distinct', in the words of the Chalcedonian formula, like Christ in his divine and human natures. Perhaps the importance of polyphony in music lies in the fact that it is a musical reflection of this Christological truth, and that it is therefore an essential element in the Christian life. All this occurred to me after you were here. Can you see what I'm driving at? I wanted to tell you that we

131]

must have a good, clear *cantus firmus*. Without it there can be no full or perfect sound, but with it the counterpoint has a firm support and cannot get out of tune or fade out, yet is always a perfect whole in its own right. Only a polyphony of this kind can give life a wholeness, and at the same time assure us that nothing can go wrong so long as the *cantus firmus* is kept going. Perhaps your leave and the separation which lies ahead will be easier for you to bear. Please do not fear or hate separation if it should come, with all its attendant perils, but pin your faith on the *cantus firmus*.—I don't know if I have made myself clear, but one speaks so seldom of such things....

May 21st 1944

I have put the date at the head of this letter as my share in the christening and all the preparations for it. At the same moment the siren went off, and I'm now sitting in the guard-room and hoping you won't have an air raid on this day of all days. What times we live in! What a baptism! And how much we shall have to look back on in years to come! All that matters is that we should make proper use of these memories and turn them to spiritual account. That will make them harder, clearer and more defiant, which is a good thing. There is no place for sentimentality on a day like this. If in the middle of an air raid God sends forth the gospel summons into his Kingdom in Holy Baptism, that will be a clear sign of the nature and purpose of that Kingdom. For it is a Kingdom stronger than war and danger, a Kingdom of power and might, signifying to some eternal terror and judgement, to others eternal joy and righteousness, not a Kingdom of the heart, but one as wide as the earth, not transitory, but eternal, a Kingdom which makes a way for itself and summons men to itself to prepare its way, a Kingdom worthy of our life's devotion. The shooting is just starting, but it doesn't look as though it's going to be too bad to-day. How I should love to hear you preaching in a few hours' time! At eight this morning I heard a choral performance of *Was Gott tut, das ist wohlgetan* —a good beginning for the day. As I listened I thought of

[132

you. I hadn't heard an organ for a long time, and its clear tone was like a refuge in time of trouble.

I suppose you will be making an after-dinner speech, and thinking of me as you do so. I should love to hear you. The very fact that we so rarely say such words to one another makes one yearn for them from time to time. Do you understand that? Perhaps absence makes one feel it all the more strongly. I used to take such things for granted, and I do so still, in spite of everything.

The subject of polyphony is still pursuing me. I was thinking to-day how painful it is without you, and it occurred to me how pain and joy are also part of the polyphony of life, and that they can exist independently side by side.

All clear! I'm so glad for your sake. I have two sprigs of lilac on my desk: someone brought them for me to-day, touching of them, wasn't it? I have also put the photos you brought in front of me, and am gazing at the baby who is being baptized to-day. I think he's lovely, and if he takes after me in looks, I only hope he will be as free from toothache and headache as I am, and be blessed with my leg muscles and sensitive gums—though that can sometimes be a disadvantage. For other things he can do better elsewhere. . . . He has also inherited the best thing about me, my name. I have always been satisfied with it, and in my younger days I was actually proud of it. Believe me, I shall always be a good godfather to him and do all I can to help him. In fact, I don't believe he could have a better one!

If war seems to you to spell nothing else but death, you are certainly not doing justice to the manifold ways of God. We have all our appointed hour of death, and it will always find us wherever we go. And we must be ready for it. But

> *He knows ten thousand ways*
> *To save us from death's power.*
> *He gives us food and meat*
> *A boon in famine's hour.*

—that's something we must never forget. I am sending you a letter for you to give to Niebuhr, in case the worst comes true.[1] We must also fix a rendezvous. Later on I have no doubt we shall be able to keep in touch through N. and Uncle George.[2]

THOUGHTS ON THE BAPTISM
OF D.W.R.

You are the first of a new generation in our family, and therefore the oldest representative of your generation. You will have the priceless advantage of spending a good part of your life with the third and fourth generation that went before you. Your great-grandfather will be able to tell you from his own memories of people who were born in the eighteenth century, and some day, long after 2000 A.D. you will be a living bridge for more than 250 years' oral tradition, though of course with Jacob's proviso, 'If God will and we live'. So your birth provides a suitable occasion to ponder on the vicissitudes of history and to try to scan the outlines of the future.

★ ★ ★

The three names you bear are reminders of three houses which are most intimately connected with your life, and which should remain so. Your grandfather on your father's side lived in a country parsonage. A simple, healthy life, with wide intellectual interests, a zest for life's little pleasures, a natural and ingenuous companionship with ordinary folk, a capacity for self-help in practical things, a modesty grounded in spiritual contentment—these are the earthly values which were at home in the country parsonage, values you will meet in your father. Whatever may betide you, they will always help you to live together with others, to achieve real success and inner happiness.

The urban middle class culture embodied in the home of your mother's parents stands for pride in public service, intellectual achievement and leadership, a deep rooted sense of duty towards a noble heritage and cultural tradition. This will

[1] In case the Editor should be taken prisoner of war.
[2] The Bishop of Chichester.

give you, even before you are aware of it, a way of thinking and acting which you will never lose without being untrue to yourself.

It was a kindly thought of your parents that you should be known by the name of your great-uncle, the Vicar of your father's parish and a great friend of his, who at the moment is sharing the fate of many other good Germans and Protestant Christians, and who therefore has only been able to participate at a distance in your parents' wedding and in your own birth and baptism, but who looks forward to your future with great confidence and cheerful hope. He is striving to keep up the spirit he sees embodied in his parents' home—your great-grandparents, so far as he understands it. He takes it as a good omen for your future that it was in this house that your parents got to know each other, and hopes that sometime you too will be grateful for the spirit of this house, and draw inspiration from it yourself. By the time you are grown up, the old country parsonage and the old town villa will belong to a vanished world. But the old spirit will still be there, and will assume new forms, after a time of neglect and weakness, of withdrawal and recovery, of preservation and convalescence. To be deeply rooted in the soil makes life harder, but it also enriches it and gives it vigour. There are certain fundamental truths about human life to which men will always return sooner or later. So there is no need to hurry: we must be able to wait. 'God seeketh again that which is passed away' (Ecclesiastes 3.15).

In the revolutionary times ahead it will be a priceless gift to know the security of a good home. It will provide a bulwark against all dangers from within and from without. The time when children rebelled in arrogance against their parents will be past. Children will be drawn for shelter to their parents, and in their home they will seek counsel, peace and light. It is your fortune to have parents who know by experience what it means to have a parental home in time of trouble. Amid the general impoverishment of culture you will find your parents' home a storehouse of spiritual values and a source of intellectual stimulation. Music, as understood and practised by your

135]

parents, will dissolve your perplexities and purify your character and emotions, and in time of anxiety and sorrow will help you to keep going a ground bass of joy. Your parents will soon be teaching you to help yourself and never to be afraid of soiling your hands. The piety of your home will not be noisy or loquacious, but you will be brought up to say your prayers and to fear God above all things, to love him and to do the will of Jesus Christ. 'My son, keep the commandments of thy father, And forsake not the law of thy mother: Bind them continually upon thy heart, Tie them about thy neck. When thou walkest, it shall watch over thee: When thou sleepest it shall lead thee: And when thou wakest, it shall talk with thee' (Proverbs 6.20-22). 'To-day is salvation come to this house' (Luke 19.9).

★   ★   ★

It would be much the best thing if you were brought up in the country. But it will be a very different countryside from that in which your father was brought up. People used to think that the big cities offered the fullest kind of life, and pleasure in abundance. They used to flock to them like pilgrims to a feast. But now these cities have brought death upon themselves, and women and children have fled from them in terror. The age of big cities on our continent seems to have come to an end. The Bible tells us that Cain was the first city dweller. A world metropolis may survive here and there, but their brilliance, alluring though it may be, will have an air of uncanniness about it, for us Europeans at any rate. This flight from the city will bring tremendous changes to the countryside. The tranquillity and remoteness of country life were already being undermined by the advent of the radio, the car and the telephone, and by the spread of bureaucracy into practically every department of life. And now that millions who can no longer endure the totalitarian claims of city life are flocking to the land, now that industries are being dispersed in rural areas, the urbanizing of the countryside will proceed apace, and the whole pattern of life there will be revolutionized. The village as it was thirty years ago no more exists to-day than the idyllic isles of the southern seas. Much as he needs solitude and peace, a man will find them very difficult to come by. But it will be an advantage amid all these changes to have beneath one's feet a few inches of soil from which to draw the resources for a new, natural, unpretentious and contented day's work and evening's leisure.

'But godliness with contentment is great gain . . . but having food and covering, we shall therewith be content' (I Timothy 6.6f.). 'Give me neither poverty nor riches: Feed me with the food that is needful for me: Lest I be full, and deny thee, and say, Who is the Lord? Or lest I be poor, and steal, And use profanely the name of my God' (Proverbs 30.8f.). 'Flee out of the midst of Babylon, and save every man his life; be not cut off in her iniquity' (Jeremiah 1.6).

★   ★   ★

We have grown up in a society which believed that every man had the right to plan his own life. There was, we were taught, a purpose in life, and it was every man's duty to accept that purpose resolutely, and pursue it to the best of his powers. Since then however we have learnt that it is impossible to plan even for one day ahead, that all our work may be destroyed overnight, and that our life, compared with our parents', has become formless and fragmentary. Despite everything, however, I can only say I should not have chosen to live in any other age than our own, though it is so regardless of our external fortunes. Never have we realized, as we do to-day, how the world lies under the wrath and grace of God. In Jeremiah 45 we read: 'Thus saith the Lord: Behold, that which I have built will I break down, and that which I planted I will pluck up; and this in the whole land. And seekest thou great things for thyself? seek them not: for behold, I will bring evil upon all flesh, saith the Lord: but thy life will I give unto thee for a prey whither thou goest.' If we can save our souls unscathed from the débris of civilization, let us be satisfied with that. If the Creator destoys his own handiwork, what right have we to lament over the destruction of ours? The task laid upon our generation is not the indulgence of lofty ambitions, but the saving of ourselves alive out of the débris, as a brand plucked from the burning. 'Keep thy heart with all diligence; for out of it are the issues of life' (Proverbs 4.23). We shall have to keep our lives going rather than shape them, to endure, rather than forge ahead. But we do want to preserve an heritage for you, the rising generation, so that you will have the resources for building a new and better world.

*   *   *

We have spent too much time thinking, supposing that if only we weigh every possibility in advance, everything will somehow happen automatically. We have learnt a bit too late in the day that action springs not from thought, but from a readiness for responsibility. For you thought and action will have a new relationship. Your thinking will be confined to your responsibilities in action. With us thought was often the luxury of the looker-on; with you it will be entirely subordinated to action. 'Not everyone that saith unto me, Lord, Lord, shall enter into the kingdom of heaven; but he that doeth the will of my Father which is in heaven' (Matthew 7.21).

*   *   *

To-day we have almost succeeded in banishing pain from our lives. To be as free from pain as possible had become one of our unconscious ideals. Nicety of feeling, sensitivity to our own and other people's pain—these things are at once the strength and the weakness of our way of life. From the very outset your generation will be tougher and closer to real life, for you will have had to endure privation and pain, and your patience will have been sorely tried. 'It is good for a man that he bear the yoke in his youth' (Lamentations 3.27).

*   *   *

We believed that reason and justice were the key to success, and where both failed, we felt we were at the end of our tether. We have constantly exaggerated the importance of reason and justice in the historical process. You are growing up during a world war which ninety per cent. of the human race did not want, yet for which they have to forfeit goods and

[138

life. So you are learning from childhood that the world is controlled by forces against which reason is powerless. This knowledge will enable you to cope with these powers more soberly and effectively. Again, in our lives the 'enemy' had no substantial reality. You know that you have enemies and friends, and you know what both can mean in life. You are learning from the cradle how to deal with your enemy, which is something we never knew, and you are learning to put unreserved trust in your friends. 'Is there not a warfare to man upon earth?' (Job 7.1). 'Blessed be the Lord my strength: who teacheth my hands to war and my fingers to fight. My hope and my fortress, my castle and deliverer, my defender in whom I trust' (Psalm 144.1f.). 'There is a friend that sticketh closer than a brother' (Proverbs 18.24).

★　　★　　★

Are we moving towards an age of colossal organizations and collective institutions, or will the desire of multitudes for small, manageable, personal relationships be satisfied? Must they be mutually exclusive? Is it not just conceivable that world organizations with their wide meshes should allow more scope for private interests? The same considerations apply to the question as to whether we are moving towards an age of the selection of the fittest, i.e. an aristocratic society, or to a uniform equality in all material and spiritual aspects of human life. Though there has been a good deal of equalization in this field, there is still a fine sensitiveness in all ranks of society for such human values as justice, success, and courage, and this is creating a new selection of potential leaders. It should not be difficult for us to forfeit our privileges, recognizing the justice of history. We may have to face events and changes which run counter to our rights and wishes. But if so, we shall not give way to bitterness and foolish pride, but consciously submit to divine judgement, and thus prove our worthiness to survive by identifying ourselves generously and unselfishly with the life of the community and the interests of our fellowmen. 'But the nation that shall bring their neck under the yoke of the king of Babylon and serve him, that nation will I let remain in their own land, saith the Lord: and they shall till it and dwell therein' (Jeremiah 27.11). 'Seek the peace of that city ... and pray unto the Lord for it' (Jeremiah 29.7). 'Come, my people, enter thou into thy chambers and shut thy doors: hide thyself for a little moment, until the danger be overpast' (Isaiah 26.20). 'For his wrath endureth but the twinkling of an eye, and in his pleasure is life: heaviness may endure for a night, but joy cometh in the morning' (Psalm 30.5).

★   ★   ★

To-day you are being baptized as a Christian. The ancient words of the Christian proclamation will be uttered over you, and the command of Jesus to baptize will be performed over you, without your knowing anything about it. But we too are being driven back to first principles. Atonement and redemption, regeneration, the Holy Ghost, the love of our enemies, the cross and resurrection, life in Christ and Christian discipleship—all these things have become so problematic and so remote that we hardly dare any more to speak of them. In the traditional rite and ceremonies we are groping after something new and revolutionary without being able to understand it or utter it yet. That is our own fault. During these years the Church has fought for self-preservation as though it were an end in itself, and has thereby lost its chance to speak a word of reconciliation to mankind and the world at large. So our traditional language must perforce become powerless and remain silent, and our Christianity to-day will be confined to praying for and doing right by our fellow men. Christian thinking, speaking and organization must be reborn out of this praying and this action. By the time you are grown up, the form of the Church will have changed beyond recognition. We are not yet out of the melting pot, and every attempt to hasten matters will only delay the Church's conversion and purgation. It is not for us to prophesy the day, but the day will come when men will be called again to utter the word of God with such power as will change and renew the world. It will be a new language, which will horrify men, and yet overwhelm them by its power. It will be the language of a new righteous-

[140

ness and truth, a language which proclaims the peace of God with men and the advent of his kingdom. 'And (they) shall fear and tremble for all the good and for all the peace that I procure unto it' (Jeremiah 33.9). Until then the Christian cause will be a silent and hidden affair, but there will be those who pray and do right and wait for God's own time. 'The path of the righteous is as a shining light, That shineth more and more unto the perfect day' (Proverbs 4.18).

May 24th 1944

. . . On the duties of godparents. In the old books the godparents often played, an important part in the child's life. Growing children frequently require sympathy, kindliness and advice from adults other than their parents. The god-parents are the people chosen by the parents for this function. The godparent has the right to give good advice, the parents to command. . . .

. . . I am reading with great interest Weizsäcker's book about the 'physical picture of the world' and hope to get a lot from it for my own work. If only there was some chance of an interchange of ideas. . . .

May 25th 1944

I hope that despite the alarms you are enjoying the peace and beauty of these warm, summer-like Whitsun days. Gradu-ally one acquires an inner detachment from the dangers that beset us. Detachment however seems too negative, artificial and stoic a word to use. Rather, we assimilate these dangers into the wholeness of our life. I have repeatedly observed here how few there are who can make room for conflicting emotions at the same time. When the bombers come, they are all fear; when there is something good to eat, they are all greed; when they are disappointed they are all despair; when they are successful, they can think of nothing else. They miss the fullness of life and the wholeness of an independent existence. Everything subjective and objective is dissolved for them into fragments. By contrast, Christianity plunges us into many different dimensions of life simultaneously. We can make room in our hearts, to some extent at least, for God and the whole world. We weep with them that weep, and rejoice with them that do rejoice. We are afraid (I was again interrupted by the alarm, and am now sitting out of doors enjoying the sun) for our life, but at the same time we must think of things more important than life itself. When an alarm goes off, for example, we have other things to think about than anxiety for our own safety; we have, e.g. to help others around us to keep calm. The moment that happens, the whole picture is changed. Life is not compressed into a single dimension, but is kept multi-dimensional and polyphonous. What a deliverance it is to be able to *think*, and in thinking to preserve this multi-dimensionality. When people tremble at an impending air-raid, I have almost made it a rule to tell them how much worse it would be for a small town. We have to keep men out of their one-track minds. That is a sort of pre-paration for faith, although it is only faith itself that can make possible a multi-dimensional life, and enable us to keep even this Whitsun despite the alarms.

At first I was disconcerted, and not a little grieved to have no letters this Whitsun. But I said to myself it was perhaps a sign that no one was worrying about me. It's strange how we like others to be anxious about us, a little bit at any rate.

Weizsäcker's book on the world view of physics is still keeping me busy. It has brought home to me how wrong it is to use God as a stop-gap for the incompleteness of our know-ledge. For the frontiers of knowledge are inevitably being pushed back further and further, which means that you only think of God as a stop-gap. He also is being pushed back further and further, and is in more or less continuous retreat. We should find God in what we do know, not in what we don't; not in outstanding problems, but in those we have already solved. This is true not only for the relation between Christianity and science, but also for wider human problems such as guilt, suffering and death. It is possible nowadays to find answers to these problems which leave God right out of the picture. It just isn't true to say that Christianity alone

[142

has the answers. In fact the Christian answers are no more conclusive or compelling than any of the others. Once more, God cannot be used as a stop-gap. We must not wait until we are at the end of our tether: he must be found at the centre of life: in life, and not only in death; in health and vigour, and not only in suffering; in activity, and not only in sin. The ground for this lies in the revelation of God in Christ. Christ is the centre of life, and in no sense did he come to answer our unsolved problems. From the centre of life certain questions are seen to be wholly irrelevant, and so are the answers commonly given to them—I am thinking for example of the judgement pronounced on the friends of Job. In Christ there are no Christian problems. Enough of this; I have just been disturbed again.

May 30th 1944 Evening

I am sitting upstairs by myself. All is quiet in the house: outside a few birds are still singing, and I can even hear the cuckoo in the distance. I find these long, warm evenings rather trying—it's the second time I have had to live through them here. I long to be outside, and if I weren't such a rational person, I might do something foolish. I wonder if we have become too rational? When you have deliberately suppressed every desire for so long, it burns you up inside, or else you get so bottled up that one day there is a terrific explosion. The only alternative is the achievement of complete selflessness. I know better than anyone else that that has not happened to me. I expect you will say it's wrong to suppress one's desires, and you would be quite right. . . . So I seek diversion in thinking and writing letters . . . and curb my desires as a measure of self-protection. I know it sounds paradoxical, but it would be more selfless if I had no fear of my desires, but could give them free rein—but that would be very difficult. Just now I happened to hear Solveig's song on the wireless up in the guard-room. It quite got hold of me. To wait loyally a whole life time—that is triumphing over the hostility of space, that is, separation, and of time, that is, the past. Don't you agree that loyalty like this is the only road to

143]

happiness, and that disloyalty is the source of unhappiness? Well, I'm off to bed now, in case we get another disturbed night. Good night.

June 2nd 1944

While you were in Italy I wrote about the Song of Songs. I must say, I prefer to read it as an ordinary love poem, which is probably the best christological exposition too. I must ponder further on Ephesians 5. I hope you've found my reflections on Bultmann, if they haven't gone astray.

June 5th 1944

I don't see any point in my not telling you I have occasion-ally felt the urge to write poetry. You are the first person I've mentioned it to. So I'm sending you a sample, first because I think it's silly to have any secrets from you, and then because I thought I would like to give you a pleasant surprise for your journey, and lastly because the theme of it is very much in your thoughts at the moment, and what I am trying to say may perhaps ring a bell in your mind. This dialogue with the past, this attempt to hold it fast and recover it, and above all the fear of losing it, is the almost daily accompaniment of my life here, and sometimes, especially after brief visits, followed as they nearly always are by long partings, it becomes a theme with variations. To take leave of others, and to live on past memories—it makes no difference whether it was yesterday or years ago, they soon melt into one—is my ever-recurring duty, and you yourself once wrote, that saying good-bye went very much against the grain. In this attempt of mine the crucial part is the last few lines. I'm inclined to think it is rather too short—what do you think? Strangely enough, the lines came out as rhymes of their own accord. The whole thing was composed in a few hours, and I have made no attempt to polish it up. . . . Perhaps I shall suppress this urge another time, and spend my time more profitably on other things. But I want to be guided by your opinion. If you like, I'll send you some further samples for your inspection.

[144

June 6th 1944
(The Normandy Landing)

My sole excuse for dashing off this note and my kind regards is that I want us to share this day together. It did not come as a surprise, yet things always turn out differently from what we expect. To-day's text takes us to the heart of the Gospel—redemption—and that is the key word to it all. Let us face the weeks ahead in faith and assurance, so far as the general future is concerned, and let us entrust your way and all our ways to God. Χάρις καὶ εἰρήνη!

June 8th 1944

I daresay, all things considered, you went off with a much lighter heart than you had feared at first. We had put off our meeting again from Christmas to Easter, then from Easter to Whitsun; first one feast passed then another. But the next feast is sure to be ours; I have no doubt about that now.

You have asked so many important questions on the subjects that have been occupying me lately, that I should be happy if I could answer them all myself. But I'm afraid the whole thing is very much in the initial stages. As usual, I am led on more by an instinctive feeling for the questions which are bound to crop up rather than by any conclusions I have reached already. I will try to define my position from the historical angle.

The movement beginning about the thirteenth century (I am not going to get involved in any arguments about the exact date) towards the autonomy of man (under which head I place the discovery of the laws by which the world lives and manages in science, social and political affairs, art, ethics and religion) has in our time reached a certain completion. Man has learned to cope with all questions of importance without recourse to God as a working hypothesis. In questions concerning science, art, and even ethics, this has become an understood thing which one scarcely dares to tilt at any more. But for the last hundred years or so it has been increasingly

145]

God no longer necessary
No pos of proving/demonst
exist of Θ in any way

true of religious questions also: it is becoming evident that everything gets along without 'God', and just as well as before. As in the scientific field, so in human affairs generally, what we call 'God' is being more and more edged out of life, losing more and more ground.

Catholic and Protestant historians are agreed that it is in this development that the great defection from God, from Christ, is to be discerned, and the more they bring in and make use of God and Christ in opposition to this trend, the more the trend itself considers itself to be anti-Christian. The world which has attained to a realization of itself and of the laws which govern its existence is so sure of itself that we become frightened. False starts and failures do not make the world deviate from the path and development it is following; they are accepted with fortitude and detachment as part of the bargain, and even an event like the present war is no exception. Christian apologetic has taken the most varying forms of opposition to this self-assurance. Efforts are made to prove to a world thus come of age that it cannot live without the tutelage of 'God'. Even though there has been surrender on all secular problems, there still remain the so-called ultimate questions—death, guilt—on which only 'God' can furnish an answer, and which are the reason why God and the Church and the pastor are needed. Thus we live, to some extent, by these ultimate questions of humanity. But what if one day they no longer exist as such, if they too can be answered without 'God'? We have of course the secularized off-shoots of Christian theology, the existentialist philosophers and the psychotherapists, who demonstrate to secure, contented, happy mankind that it is really unhappy and desperate, and merely unwilling to realize that it is in severe straits it knows nothing at all about, from which only they can rescue it. Wherever there is health, strength, security, simplicity, they spy luscious fruit to gnaw at or to lay their pernicious eggs in. They make it their object first of all to drive men to inward despair, and then it is all theirs. That is secularized methodism. And whom does it touch? A small number of intellectuals, of degenerates, of people who regard themselves as the most important thing in

[146

the world and hence like looking after themselves. The ordinary man who spends his everyday life at work, and with his family, and of course with all kinds of hobbies and other interests too, is not affected. He has neither time nor inclination for thinking about his intellectual despair and regarding his modest share of happiness as a trial, a trouble or a disaster.

The attack by Christian apologetic upon the adulthood of the world I consider to be in the first place pointless, in the second ignoble, and in the third un-Christian. Pointless, because it looks to me like an attempt to put a grown-up man back into adolescence, i.e. to make him dependent on things on which he is not in fact dependent any more, thrusting him back into the midst of problems which are in fact not problems for him any more. Ignoble, because this amounts to an effort to exploit the weakness of man for purposes alien to him and not freely subscribed to by him. Un-Christian, because for Christ himself is being substituted one particular stage in the religiousness of man, i.e. a human law. Of this more later.

But first a word or two on the historical situation. The question is, Christ and the newly matured world. It was the weak point of liberal theology that it allowed the world the right to assign Christ his place in that world: in the dispute between Christ and the world it accepted the comparatively clement peace dictated by the world. It was its strong point that it did not seek to put back the clock, and genuinely accepted the battle (Troeltsch), even though this came to an end with its overthrow.

Overthrow was succeeded by capitulation and an attempt at a completely fresh start based on consideration of the Bible and Reformation fundamentals of the faith. Heim sought, along pietist and methodist lines, to convince individual man that he was faced with the alternative 'either despair or Jesus'. He gained 'hearts'. Althaus, carrying forward the modern and positive line with a strong confessional emphasis, endeavoured to wring from the world a place for Lutheran teaching (ministry) and Lutheran worship, and otherwise left the world to its own devices. Tillich set out to interpret the evolution of the world itself—against its will—in a religious sense, to give it

147]

its whole shape through religion. That was very courageous of
him, but the world unseated him and went on by itself: he
too sought to understand the world better than it understood
itself, but it felt entirely *mis*understood, and rejected the
imputation. (Of course the world does need to be understood
better than it understands itself, but not 'religiously', as the
religious socialists desired.) Barth was the first to realize the
mistake that all these efforts (which were all unintentionally
sailing in the channel of liberal theology) were making in having
as their objective the clearing of a space for religion in the
world or against the world.

He called the God of Jesus Christ into the lists against
religion, '*pneuma* against *sarx*'. That was and is his greatest service (the second edition of his Epistle to the Romans, in spite
of all its neo-Kantian shavings). Through his later dogmatics,
he enabled the Church to effect this distinction in principle all
along the line. It was not that he subsequently, as is often
claimed, failed in ethics, for his ethical observations—so far as he
has made any—are just as significant as his dogmatic ones; it was
that he gave no concrete guidance, either in dogmatics or in
ethics, on the non-religious interpretation of theological concepts. There lies his limitation, and because of it his theology
of revelation becomes positivist, a 'positivism of revelation',
as I put it.

The Confessing Church has to a great extent forgotten all
about the Barthian approach, and lapsed from positivism into
conservative restoration. The important thing about that
Church is that it carries on the great concepts of Christian
theology, but that seems all it will do. There are, certainly,
in these concepts the elements of genuine prophetic quality
(under which head come both the claim to truth and the
mercy you mention) and of genuine worship, and to that
extent the message of the Confessing Church meets only with
attention, hearing and rejection. But they both remain unex-
plained and remote, because there is no interpretation of them.

People like, for instance, Schütz, or the Oxford Group, or
the Berneucheners, who miss the 'movement' and 'life', are dangerous reactionaries, retrogressive because they go straight

[148

back behind the approach of revelation theology and seek for 'religious' renewal. They simply do not understand the problem at all, and what they say is entirely beside the point. There is no future for them (though the Oxford people would have the biggest chance if they were not so completely devoid of biblical substance).

Bultmann would seem to have felt Barth's limitations in some way, but he misconstrues them in the light of liberal theology, and hence goes off into the typical liberal reduction process (the 'mythological' elements of Christianity are dropped, and Christianity is reduced to its 'essence'). I am of the view that the full content, including the mythological concepts, must be maintained. The New Testament is not a mythological garbing of the universal truth; this mythology (resurrection and so on) is the thing itself—but the concepts must be interpreted in such a way as not to make religion a pre-condition of faith (cf. circumcision in St. Paul). Not until that is achieved will, in my opinion, liberal theology be overcome (and even Barth is still dominated by it, though negatively), and, at the same time, the question it raises be genuinely taken up and answered—which is not the case in the positivism of revelation maintained by the Confessing Church.

The world's coming of age is then no longer an occasion for polemics and apologetics, but it is really better understood than it understands itself, namely on the basis of the Gospel, and in the light of Christ.

You ask whether this leaves any room for the Church, or has it gone for good? And again, did not Jesus himself use distress as his point of contact with men, whether as a consequence the 'methodism' I have so frowned upon is not right after all? I'm breaking off here, and will write more to-morrow.

June 21st 1944

Now you are somewhere searching for your unit, and I hope that when you reach it you will find some letters to greet you there, that is, assuming your old field post number is still correct. All I want to do to-day is to send you my best wishes.

I daren't enclose the next instalments of theology or poetry for fear they go astray. As soon as I am certain about your address, there will be some more to follow. I am most grateful for your comments and criticisms on the poem. I feel rather at sea with these new children of mine, and haven't any standards to judge them by.

This morning we had one of the worst air raids so far. My room was filled with a cloud of smoke which hung about for several hours. The whole city was shrouded in it, and it was so dark I almost switched the light on. Have just heard that all's well at home.

It often seems hard to have to spend a second summer here. But it's not for us to choose where we are to be. So we must keep on trying to banish those petty thoughts that irritate, and win our way through to those great thoughts which are a source of inspiration. Just now I'm reading an outstanding book by W. F. Otto, the Classics man at Koenigsberg. It's about the Greek Gods. To quote from his closing words, it is about 'this world of faith, which sprang from the wealth and depth of human existence, rather than from its cares and longings'. I wonder if you will understand me when I say I find something attractive in this theme and the way it is treated in this book. In fact, I find these gods—*horribile dictu*—less offensive when treated like this than certain brands of Christianity! I believe I could pretty nearly claim these gods for Christ. This book is most helpful for my present theological reflections.

SORROW AND JOY

Sorrow and Joy:
striking suddenly on our startled senses
seem, at the first approach, all but impossible
of just distinction one from the other:
even as frost and heat at the first keen contact
burn us alike.

Joy and Sorrow,
hurled from the height of heaven in meteor fashion,
flash in an arc of shining menace o'er us.
Those they touch are left
stricken amid the fragments
of their colourless, usual lives.

Imperturbable, mighty,
ruinous and compelling,
Sorrow and Joy
—summoned or all unsought for—
processionally enter.
Those they encounter
they transfigure, investing them
with strange gravity
and a spirit of worship.

Joy is rich in fears:
Sorrow has its sweetness.
Undistinguishable from each other
they approach us from eternity,
equally potent in their power and terror.

From every quarter
mortals come hurrying:
part envious, part awe-struck,
swarming, and peering
into the portent;
where the mystery sent from above us
is transmuting into the inevitable
order of earthly human drama.

What then is Joy? What then is Sorrow?
Time alone can decide between them,
when the immediate poignant happening
lengthens out to continuous wearisome suffering;
when the laboured creeping moments of daylight
slowly uncover the fulness of our disaster
Sorrow's unmistakable features.

Then do most of our kind
sated, if only by the monotony
of unrelieved unhappiness,
turn away from the drama, disillusioned,
uncompassionate.

O ye mothers, and loved ones—then, ah, then
comes your hour, the hour for true devotion.
Then your hour comes, ye friends and brothers!
Loyal hearts can change the face of Sorrow,
softly encircle it with love's most gentle
unearthly radiance.

LETTERS TO A FRIEND

Though I haven't the least idea whether the post is reaching you, or when it is likely to arrive, I'm still addressing this by your old field post number. I should prefer to wait till I hear from you before resuming my theological reflections, and the same goes for the verses, which are more suitable for an evening's talk than for a long journey by post. That is particularly true of my latest effort, a somewhat lengthy effusion on my impressions of prison life.[1]

At the moment I am engaged in expounding the first three commandments. I find No. 2 particularly difficult. The usual interpretation of idolatry as 'riches, debauchery and desire' seems unbiblical. That is a bit of moralizing. Idols are objects of worship, and idolatry implies that people still worship something. The truth is, we've given up worshipping everything, even idols. In fact, we are absolute nihilists.

To resume our reflections on the Old Testament. Unlike the other oriental religions the faith of the Old Testament is not a religion of salvation. Christianity, it is true, has always been regarded as a religion of salvation. But isn't this a cardinal error, which divorces Christ from the Old Testament and interprets him in the light of the myths of salvation? Of course it could be urged that under Egyptian and later, Babylonian influence, the idea of salvation became just as prominent in the Old Testament—e.g. Deutero-Isaiah. The answer is, the Old Testament speaks of *historical* redemption, i.e. redemption on this side of death, whereas the myths of salvation are concerned to offer men deliverance from death. Israel is redeemed out of Egypt in order to live before God on earth. The salvation myths deny history in the interests of an eternity after death. Sheol and Hades are no metaphysical theories, but images which imply that the past, while it still exists, has only a shadowy existence in the present. It is said that the distinctive feature of Christianity is its proclamation of the resurrection

[1] *Nächtliche Stimmen*, Haus und Schule Verlag, Berlin.

hope, and that this means the establishment of a genuine religion of salvation, in the sense of release from this world. The emphasis falls upon the far side of the boundary drawn by death. But this seems to me to be just the mistake and the danger. Salvation means salvation from cares and need, from fears and longing, from sin and death into a better world beyond the grave. But is this really the distinctive feature of Christianity as proclaimed in the Gospels and St. Paul? I am sure it is not. The difference between the Christian hope of resurrection and a mythological hope is that the Christian hope sends a man back to his life on earth in a wholly new way which is even more sharply defined than it is in the Old Testament.

The Christian, unlike the devotees of the salvation myths, does not need a last refuge in the eternal from earthly tasks and difficulties. But like Christ himself ('My God, my God, why hast thou forsaken me?') he must drink the earthly cup to the lees, and only in his doing that is the crucified and risen Lord with him, and he crucified and risen with Christ. This world must not be prematurely written off. In this the Old and New Testaments are at one. Myths of salvation arise from human experiences of the boundary situation. Christ takes hold of a man in the centre of his life.

You see how my thoughts are constantly revolving round the same theme. I must now collect some evidence from the New Testament to support my contentions, in the hope of sending it on later.

I read in the paper that you are having tropical heat in Italy—you poor man! It reminds me of August 1936. Psalm 121.6!

June 30th 1944

We had a really hot summer's day here to-day, but I could only enjoy it with mixed feelings, for I can't help thinking of what you are having to go through. I can just imagine you sitting down somewhere covered in dust, hot and tired, and perhaps without any chance of washing or refreshment. No doubt you sometimes almost loathe the sun. And yet you know, I should like to feel the full force of it again, burning

the skin and making the whole frame glow, and reminding me
that I have still got a body. If only I could get tired of the sun,
instead of books and thoughts! I should love to have my
animal existence awakened, not the kind that degrades a man,
but the sort that delivers him from the stuffiness and spurious-
ness of a purely intellectual existence and makes him purer and
happier. I should love not just to see the sun and have only a
little of it, but to experience it bodily. Modern sun-worship
is romantic nonsense. It gets intoxicated over the sunrise and
sunset, it knows something about the power of the sun, but
does not know it as a reality, but only as a symbol. It cannot
understand the way the ancients worshipped it as a god: for
that it is necessary to appreciate not only its light and colour,
but also its heat. The hot countries, from the Mediterranean
to India and Central America, have been the cradle of genuine
culture. The colder lands have lived and thrived on the
creativeness of the others, and such originality as they have is
confined to the field of technics, which in the last resort serves
the material needs of life rather than the mind. Is that why we
find the hot countries so attractive? And do not such thoughts
do something to compensate for the discomforts of the heat?
No doubt you will think that's neither here nor there and you
are simply longing to get out of that hell, back to Grunewald
and a glass of Berlin beer. I can well remember how I longed
to get out of Italy in June 1923, and I only got my breath back
again on a day's ramble in the Black Forest, when it was pouring
cats and dogs. And there wasn't a war on then, and all I had to
do was to enjoy it. I can also remember your horror in August
1936 when I wanted us to push on to Naples. How are you
standing up to it now? That time before we could never have
survived without the 'expresso', and K., to my youthful
annoyance, threw away a lot of money on it. Beside that, we
took a coach even for the shortest distances, and consumed vast
quantities of *granitos* and *cassatas* on the way. I have just had
the joyful news that you have written and that you have kept
your old field post number, from which I conclude you have
found your old unit again. You can't imagine how reassured
I am, relatively, at any rate.

A few hours since Uncle Paul[1] called here to make personal enquiries about my welfare. I can't help laughing at the way everyone goes about flapping his wings and tries to outdo everybody else in undignified ways. There are a few notable exceptions, of course. It is painful but many of them are in such a state now that they can't help it.

Let me carry on a bit with the theological reflections I started on a little while ago. I began by saying that God is being increasingly edged out of the world, now that it has come of age. Knowledge and life are thought to be perfectly possible without him. Ever since Kant, he has been relegated to the realm beyond experience.

Theology has endeavoured to produce an apologetic to meet this development, engaging in futile rear-guard actions against Darwinism, etc. At other times it has accommodated itself to this development by restricting God to the so-called last questions as a kind of *Deus ex machina*. God thus became the answer to life's problems, the solution of its distresses and conflicts. As a result, if anyone had no such difficulties, if he refused to identify himself in sympathy with those who had, it was no good trying to win him for God. The only way of getting at him was to show that he had all these problems, needs and conflicts without being aware of it or owning up to it. Existentialist philosophy and pyschotherapy have both been pretty clever at this sort of thing. It is then possible to talk to a man about God, and methodism can celebrate its triumph. If however it does not come off, if a man won't see that his happiness is really damnation, his health sickness, his vigour and vitality despair; if he won't call them what they really are, the theologian is at his wits' end. He must be a hardened sinner of a particularly vicious type. If not, he is a case of bourgeois complacency, and the one is as far from salvation as the other.

You see, this is the attitude I am contending against. When Jesus blessed sinners, they were real sinners, but Jesus did not make every man a sinner first. He called them out of their sin,

[1] General Paul von Hase, Commandant of Berlin, who was condemned to death a few weeks later by the People's Court, and executed.

not into their sin. Of course encounter with Jesus meant the reversal of all human values. So it was in the conversion of St. Paul, though in his case the knowledge of sin preceded his encounter with Jesus. Of course Jesus took to himself the dregs of human society, harlots, and publicans, but never them alone, for he sought to take to himself man as such. Never did Jesus throw any doubt on a man's health, vigour or fortune, regarded in themselves, or look upon them as evil fruits. Else why did he heal the sick and restore strength to the weak? Jesus claims for himself and the kingdom of God the whole of human life in all its manifestations.

Of course I would be interrupted just now! Let me briefly summarize what I am concerned about: it is, how can we reclaim for Christ a world which has come of age?

I can't write any more to-day, or else the letter will have to wait for another week, and I don't want that to happen. More next time!

Uncle Paul has been here. He had me fetched down straight away, and stayed more than five hours. He sent for four bottles of champagne, a unique event in the annals of this establishment. I would never have dreamt he could be so nice and generous. He must have wanted to show the world what good terms he is on with me, and what he expects from the scrupulous and pedantic M. Such a spirit of independence, quite unthinkable in a civilian, was most remarkable. By the way, he told me the following story: At St. Privat a wounded ensign shouted out, 'I am wounded, long live the King!' Whereupon General von Löwenfeld, who was also wounded, retorted: 'Hold your tongue: we die here in silence.' I am curious to know what will be the outcome of his visit—I mean, what the others will think about it.

Well now, good-bye, and forgive me for breaking off. But I think you would sooner have this than nothing at all. I hope we shall all be together again early in the autumn.

July 1st 1944

Seven years ago to-day we were together at Martin's.[1]

[1] The day Martin Niemöller was arrested.

July 8th 1944

A short time ago I sent you a letter containing some very theoretical philosophizing on the subject of heat. During the past few days I've had a taste of it myself, and I'm feeling as though I were in an oven. I am wearing only a shirt I bought one day with you and a pair of shorts. But I don't complain about it, for I can imagine how much worse it must be for you, and how frivolous my remarks on the subject must have seemed to you. So let me try and squeeze a few thoughts out of my sweating brain, and let you have them. Who knows, perhaps we shan't have to write much longer! The other day I came across a wonderful phrase in Euripides, in a scene of reunion after long absence: 'So then, to meet again is a god.'

Now a few more thoughts on our theme. Marshalling the biblical evidence requires more lucidity and concentration than I am capable of at the moment. Let's wait a few more days until its gets cooler. I haven't forgotten I owe you something about the non-religious interpretation of biblical terminology. But let me start to-day with a few preliminary observations.

When God was driven out of the world, and from the public side of human life, an attempt was made to retain him at least in the sphere of the 'personal', the 'inner life', the private life. And since every man still has a private sphere, it was thought that he was most vulnerable at this point. The secrets known by a man's valet, that is, to put it crudely, the area of his intimate life—from prayer to his sexual life—have become the hunting ground of modern psychotherapists. In this way they resemble, though quite involuntarily, the dirtiest gutter journalists. Think of the newspapers which specialize in bringing to light the most intimate details about prominent people. They practise social, financial and political blackmail on their victims: the psychotherapists practise religious blackmail. Forgive me, but I cannot say less about them.

From the sociological point of view this is a revolution from below, a revolt of inferiority. Just as the vulgar mentality is never satisfied until it has seen some highly placed personage in his bathing attire, or in other compromising situations, so

[158

it is here. There is a kind of malicious satisfaction in knowing that everyone has his weaknesses and nakednesses. In my contacts with the outcasts of society, its pariahs, I have often noticed how mistrust is the dominant motive in their judgements of other people. Every act of a person of high repute, be it never so altruistic, is suspected from the outset. Incidentally, I find such outcasts in all ranks of society. In a flower garden they grub around for the dung on which the flowers grow. The less responsible a man's life, the more easily he falls a victim to this attitude.

This irresponsibility and absence of bonds has its counterpart among the clergy in what I should call the 'priestly' snuffing around in the sins of men in order to catch them out. It is as though a beautiful house could only be known after a cobweb had been found in the furthermost corner of the cellar, or as though a good play could only be appreciated after one had seen how the actors behave off-stage. It is the same kind of thing you find in the novels of the last fifty years, which think they have only depicted their characters properly when they have described them in bed, or in films where it is thought necessary to include undressing scenes. What is clothed, veiled, pure and chaste is considered to be deceitful, disguised and impure, and in fact only shows the impurity of the writers themselves. Mistrust and suspicion as the basic attitude of men is characteristic of the revolt of inferiority.

From the theological point of view the error is twofold. First, it is thought that a man can be addressed as a sinner only after his weaknesses and meannesses have been spied out. Second, it is thought that man's essential nature consists of his inmost and most intimate background, and that is defined as his 'interior life'; and it is in these secret human places that God is now to have his domain!

On the first point it must be said that man is certainly a sinner, but not mean or common, not by a long chalk. To put the matter in the most banal way, are Goethe or Napoleon sinners because they were not always faithful husbands? It is not the sins of weakness, but the sins of strength, which matter here. It is not in the least necessary to spy out things. The

Bible never does so. (Sins of strength: in the genius, *hybris*, in the peasant, the breaking of the order of life—is the Decalogue a peasant ethic?—in the bourgeois, fear of free responsibility. Is this correct?)

On the second point it must be said that the Bible does not recognize our distinction of outer and inner. And why should it? It is always concerned with *anthropos teleios*, the *whole* man, even where, as in the Sermon on the Mount, the decalogue is pressed home to refer to inward disposition. It is quite un-biblical to suppose that a 'good intention' is enough. What matters is the whole good. The discovery of inwardness, so-called, derives from the Renaissance, from Petrarch perhaps. The 'heart' in the biblical sense is not the inward life, but the whole man in relation to God. The view that man lives just as much from outwards to inwards as from inwards to out-wards is poles apart from the view that his essential nature is to be understood from his intimate background.

This is why I am so anxious that God should not be relegated to some last secret place, but that we should frankly recognize that the world and men have come of age, that we should not speak ill of man in his worldliness, but confront him with God at his strongest point, that we should give up all our clerical subterfuges, and our regarding of psychotherapy and existentialism as precursors of God. The importunity of these people is far too unaristocratic for the Word of God to ally itself with them. The Word of God is far removed from this revolt of mistrust, this revolt from below. But it reigns.

It's high time I said something concrete on the worldly inter-pretation of the terminology of the Bible, but it's too hot!

If you want to send extracts from my letters to —— by all means do so, but I would never suggest it myself. When I write to you I am only thinking aloud in order to clarify my thoughts. You are the only person I can do that with. But please yourself. We shall soon have to be thinking of our travels together in 1940 and of my last sermon.[1]

[1] This is a code reference to East Prussia, where Hitler's headquarters were situated and where the attempt on his life was shortly to be made (20th July).

[160

July 9th. Must close for now. I'm sure we shall be meeting again soon.

July 16th 1944

I heard yesterday you had been moved again. I hope I shall soon hear how you are getting on. The historic atmosphere[1] sounds attractive enough. Ten years ago we should hardly have understood how the squabble between Emperor and Pope over the crozier and ring could lead to a first class political struggle. After all, were they not *adiaphora*? Recent experience has taught us otherwise. Whether Henry IV's pilgrimage to Canossa was honest or diplomatic, that event of 1077 is one the memory of which has burnt itself deeply in European history. It was much more effective than the Concordat of Worms, which brought the controversy to a formal conclusion in the way Henry desired. We were taught at school that the whole business was a European disaster, whereas in point of fact it is the foundation of that freedom of thought which has made Europe great.

There is little to report about myself. The other day I heard on the wireless some excerpts from the operas of Carl Orff (Carmina Burana and others). I thought they were first rate, so fresh, so clear, and so serene. He has also produced an orchestral version of Monteverdi. Did you know that? I also heard a Concerto Grosso by Handel, and once more I was astounded at the effectiveness with which he uses an extended phrase as he does in the Largo. There was something so comforting about it. Handel seems to pay far more attention to his audience than Bach does; he is more concerned about the effect of his music. That is why he so often has a façade-like effect. There is a deliberate purpose behind his music, unlike that of Bach. Is that not so?

I find the *House of the Dead* extremely interesting. It's striking what sympathy those outside have for its inhabitants—so free from moral scruples. Is not this amorality, the product of religiosity, perhaps an essential trait of this people? And may

[1] In the neighbourhood of Canossa.

it not provide a clue to more recent events? By the way I am doing as much writing and composing as much poetry as my strength allows. I have already told you that I sometimes get a chance of an evening to work as we used to in earlier days.[1] It is a source of profit and enjoyment. Otherwise there is nothing more to report. . . . I am glad K. is getting on so well. For a long time he was so depressed.[2] But I'm sure all his worries will soon be over. I very much hope so for his own sake, as well as for the whole family's.

If you have to preach a sermon in the near future, I should suggest such texts as: Psalms 62.2; 119.94a; 42.6: Jeremiah 31.3: Isaiah 41.10; 43.1: Matthew 28.20b, and confine myself to a few simple but vital thoughts. One has to live in a parish for a long time to see how Christ is 'being formed' in it (Galatians 4.19), and that is pre-eminently true of the sort of parish you are likely to have.

Now a few more thoughts on our theme. I find it's very slow going trying to work out a non-religious interpretation of biblical terminology, and it's a far bigger job than I can manage at the moment. On the historical side I should say there is *one* great development which leads to the idea of the autonomy of the world. In theology it is first discernible in Lord Herbert of Cherbury, with his assertion that reason is the sufficient instrument of religious knowledge. In ethics it first appears in Montaigne and Bodin with their substitution of moral principles for the ten commandments. In politics, Machiavelli, who emancipates politics from the tutelage of morality, and founds the doctrine of 'reasons of state'. Later, and very differently, though like Machiavelli tending towards the autonomy of human society, comes Grotius, with his international law as the law of nature, a law which would still be valid, *etsi deus non daretur*. The process is completed in philosophy. On the one hand we have the deism of Descartes, who holds that the world is a mechanism which runs on its own without any intervention of God. On the other hand there is the pantheism of Spinoza, with its identification of God with

[1] Listening to foreign broadcasts.

[2] B. is referring here to the resistance movement.

nature. In the last resort Kant is a deist, Fichte and Hegel pantheists. All along the line there is a growing tendency to assert the autonomy of man and the world.

In natural science the process seems to start with Nicolas of Cusa and Giordano Bruno with their 'heretical' doctrine of the infinity of space. The classical cosmos was finite, like the created world of the middle ages. An infinite universe, however it be conceived, is self-subsisting *etsi deus non daretur*. It is true that modern physics is not so sure as it was about the infinity of the universe, but it has not returned to the earlier conceptions of its finitude.

There is no longer any need for God as a working hypothesis, whether in morals, politics or science. Nor is there any need for such a God in religion or philosophy (Feuerbach). In the name of intellectual honesty these working hypotheses should be dropped or dispensed with as far as possible. A scientist or physician who seeks to provide edification is a hybrid.

At this point nervous souls start asking what room there is left for God now. And being ignorant of the answer they write off the whole development which has brought them to this pass. As I said in an earlier letter, various emergency exits have been devised to deal with this situation. To them must be added the *salto mortale* back to the Middle Ages, the fundamental principle of which however is heteronomy in the form of clericalism. But that is a counsel of despair, which can be purchased only at the cost of intellectual sincerity. It reminds one of the song:

> *It's a long way back to the land of childhood,*
> *But if only I knew the way!*

There isn't any such way, at any rate not at the cost of deliberately abandoning our intellectual sincerity. The only way is that of Matthew 18.3, i.e. through repentance, through *ultimate* honesty. And the only way to be honest is to recognize that we have to live in the world *etsi deus non daretur*. And this is just what we do see—before God! So our coming of age forces us to a true recognition of our situation *vis à vis* God.

163]

as tho Ɵ were not given
if 1C7 line as if

God is teaching us that we must live as men who can get along very well without him. The God who is with us is the God who forsakes us (Mark 15.34). The God who makes us live in this world without using him as a working hypothesis is the God before whom we are ever standing. Before God and with him we live without God. God allows himself to be edged out of the world and on to the cross. God is weak and powerless in the world, and that is exactly the way, the only way, in which he can be with us and help us. Matthew 8.17 makes it crystal clear that it is not by his omnipotence that Christ helps us, but by his weakness and suffering.

This is the decisive difference between Christianity and all religions. Man's religiosity makes him look in his distress to the power of God in the world; he uses God as a *Deus ex machina*. The Bible however directs him to the powerlessness and suffering of God; only a suffering God can help. To this extent we may say that the process we have described by which the world came of age was an abandonment of a false conception of God, and a clearing of the decks for the God of the Bible, who conquers power and space in the world by his weakness. This must be the starting point for our 'worldly' interpretation.

WHO AM I?

Who am I? They often tell me
I stepped from my cell's confinement
Calmly, cheerfully, firmly,
Like a squire from his country-house.
Who am I? They often tell me
I used to speak to my warders
Freely and friendly and clearly,
As though it were mine to command.
Who am I? They also tell me
I bore the days of misfortune
Equably, smilingly, proudly,
Like one accustomed to win.

Am I then really all that which other men tell of?
Or am I only what I myself know of myself?
Restless and longing and sick, like a bird in a cage,
Struggling for breath, as though hands were compressing my throat,
Yearning for colours, for flowers, for the voices of birds,
Thirsting for words of kindness, for neighbourliness,
Tossing in expectation of great events,
Powerlessly trembling for friends at an infinite distance,
Weary and empty at praying, at thinking, at making,
Faint, and ready to say farewell to it all?

Who am I? This or the other?
Am I one person to-day and to-morrow another?
Am I both at once? A hypocrite before others,
And before myself a contemptibly woebegone weakling?
Or is something within me still like a beaten army,
Fleeing in disorder from victory already achieved?

Who am I? They mock me, these lonely questions of mine.
Whoever I am, Thou knowest, O God, I am Thine!

July 18th 1944

I wonder how many of our letters have been destroyed in the raids on Munich? Did you get the one containing the two poems (*Who am I?* and *Christians and Unbelievers*)? It was just sent off that evening, and it also contained a few introductory remarks on our theological theme. The poem about Christians and Unbelievers embodies an idea you will recognize: 'Christians range themselves with God in his suffering; that is what distinguishes them from the heathen.' As Jesus asked in Gethsemane, 'Could ye not watch with me one hour?' That is the exact opposite of what the religious man expects from God. Man is challenged to participate in the sufferings of God at the hands of a godless world.

He must therefore plunge himself into the life of a godless world, without attempting to gloss over its ungodliness with a veneer of religion or trying to transfigure it. He must live a 'worldly' life and so participate in the suffering of God. He *may* live a worldly life as one emancipated from all false religions and obligations. To be a Christian does not mean to be religious in a particular way, to cultivate some particular form of ascetism (as a sinner, a penitent or a saint), but to be a man. It is not some religious act which makes a Christian what he is, but participation in the suffering of God in the life of the world.

This is *metanoia*. It is not in the first instance bothering about one's own needs, problems, sins, and fears, but allowing oneself to be caught up in the way of Christ, into the Messianic event, and thus fulfilling Isaiah 53. Therefore, 'believe in the Gospel', or in the words of St. John the Baptist, 'Behold the lamb of God that taketh away the sin of the world.' (By the way, Jeremias has recently suggested that in Aramaic the word for 'lamb' could also mean 'servant'—very appropriate, in view of Isaiah 53). This being caught up into the Messianic suffering of God in Jesus Christ takes a variety of forms in the New Testament. It appears in the call to discipleship, in Jesus' table fellowship with sinners, in conversions in the narrower sense of the word (e.g. Zacchaeus), in the act of the woman who was a sinner (Luke 7), an act which she

[166

performed without any specific confession of sin, in the healing of the sick (Matthew 8.17, see above), in Jesus' acceptance of the children. The shepherds, like the wise men from the east, stand at the crib, not as converted sinners, but because they were drawn to the crib by the star just as they were. The centurion of Capernaum (who does not make any confession of sin) is held up by Jesus as a model of faith (cf. Jairus). Jesus loves the rich young man. The eunuch (Acts 8), Cornelius (Acts 10) are anything but 'existences over the abyss'. Nathanael is an Israelite without guile (John 1.47). Finally, Joseph of Arimathaea and the women at the tomb. All that is common between them is their participation in the suffering of God in Christ. That is their faith. There is nothing of religious asceticism here. The religious act is always something partial, faith is always something whole, an act involving the whole life. Jesus does not call men to a new religion, but to life. What is the nature of that life, that participation in the powerlessness of God in the world? More about that next time, I hope.

Just one more point for to-day. When we speak of God in a non-religious way, we must not gloss over the ungodliness of the world, but expose it in a new light. Now that it has come of age, the world is more godless, and perhaps it is for that very reason nearer to God than ever before.

Forgive me putting it all so clumsily and badly. . . . We have to get up nearly every night at 1.30, which is not very good for work like this.

CHRISTIANS AND UNBELIEVERS

Men go to God when they are sore bestead,
Pray to him for succour, for his peace, for bread,
For mercy for them sick, sinning or dead:
All men do so, Christian and unbelieving.

Men go to God when he is sore bestead,
Find him poor and scorned, without shelter or bread,
Whelmed under weight of the wicked, the weak, the dead:
Christians stand by God in his hour of grieving.

God goeth to every man when sore bestead,
Feedeth body and spirit with his bread,
For Christians, heathens alike he hangeth dead:
And both alike forgiving.

July 21st 1944[1]

All I want to do to-day is to send you a short greeting. I
expect you are often thinking about us, and you are always
pleased to hear we are still alive, even if we lay aside our
theological discussion for the moment. It's true these theological problems are always occupying my mind, but there
are times when I am just content to live the life of faith without worrying about its problems. In such moods I take a
simple pleasure in the text of the day, and yesterday's and
to-day's were particularly good (July 20th: Psalm 20.8: Romans
8.31; 21.7: Psalm 23.1: John 10.24). Then I go back to Paul
Gerhardt's wonderful hymns, which never pall.

During the last year or so I have come to appreciate the
'worldliness' of Christianity as never before. The Christian is
not a *homo religiosus*, but a man, pure and simple, just as Jesus
was man, compared with John the Baptist anyhow. I don't
mean the shallow this-worldliness of the enlightened, of the
busy, the comfortable or the lascivious. It's something much
more profound than that, something in which the knowledge
of death and resurrection is ever present. I believe Luther lived
a this-worldly life in this sense. I remember talking to a young
French pastor at A. thirteen years ago. We were discussing what
our real purpose was in life. He said he would like to become
a saint. I think it is quite likely he did become one. At the
time I was very much impressed, though I disagreed with him,
and said I should prefer to have faith, or words to that effect.
For a long time I did not realize how far we were apart. I
thought I could acquire faith by trying to live a holy life, or
something like it. It was in this phase that I wrote *The Cost of
Discipleship*. To-day I can see the dangers of this book, though
I am prepared to stand by what I wrote.

[1] Written after the news of the failure of the attempt to assassinate
Hitler on the 20th July.

Later I discovered and am still discovering up to this very moment that it is only by living completely in this world that one learns to believe. One must abandon every attempt to make something of oneself, whether it be a saint, a converted sinner, a churchman (the priestly type, so-called!) a righteous man or an unrighteous one, a sick man or a healthy one. This is what I mean by worldliness—taking life in one's stride, with all its duties and problems, its successes and failures, its experiences and helplessness. It is in such a life that we throw ourselves utterly in the arms of God and participate in his sufferings in the world and watch with Christ in Gethsemane. That is faith, that is *metanoia*, and that is what makes a man and a Christian (cf. Jeremiah 45). How can success make us arrogant or failure lead us astray, when we participate in the sufferings of God by living in this world?

I think you get my meaning, though I put it so briefly. I am glad I have been able to learn it, and I know I could only have done so along the road I have travelled. So I am grateful and content with the past and the present. Perhaps you are surprised at the personal tone of this letter, but if for once I want to talk like this, to whom else should I say it? May God in his mercy lead us through these times. But above all may he lead us to himself!

I was delighted to hear from you, and glad you aren't finding it too hot. There must still be many letters from me on the way. Did we travel more or less along that way in 1936?

Good-bye. Take care of yourself and don't lose hope—we shall all meet again soon!

STATIONS ON THE ROAD
TO FREEDOM

Discipline

If you would find freedom, learn above all to discipline your senses and your soul. Be not led hither and thither by your desires and your members. Keep your spirit and your body chaste, wholly subject to you, and obediently seeking the goal that is set before you. None can learn the secret of freedom, save by discipline.

Action

To do and dare—not what you would, but what is right. Never to hesitate over what is within your power, but boldly to grasp what lies before you. Not in the flight of fancy, but only in the deed there is freedom. Away with timidity and reluctance! Out into the storm of event, sustained only by the commandment of God and your faith, and freedom will receive your spirit with exultation.

Suffering

O wondrous change! Those hands, once so strong and active, have now been bound. Helpless and forlorn, you see the end of your deed. Yet with a sigh of relief you resign your cause to a stronger hand, and are content to do so. For one brief moment you enjoyed the bliss of freedom, only to give it back to God, that he might perfect it in glory.

Death

Come now, Queen of the feasts on the road to eternal freedom! O death, cast off the grievous chains and lay low the thick walls of our mortal body and our blinded soul, that at last we may behold what here we have failed to see. O freedom, long have we sought thee in discipline and in action and in suffering. Dying, we behold thee now, and see thee in the face of God.

Dear E.

I wrote these lines in a few hours this evening. I'm afraid they are very unpolished, but perhaps you will enjoy them all the same. Please accept them as a birthday present.

From yours ever,

Dietrich

As I read these lines over in the early morning I see they need complete revision, but I'm still sending them to you as they are. After all, I don't pretend to be a poet!

July 25th 1944

I like to take every chance of writing to you, for I think you are always pleased to get a line from me. There is nothing particular to report about myself. . . . During the last few nights it has been our turn again in this district. While the bombs come crashing down, I always think how trivial it all is compared with what you are having to go through out there. I often get very cross at the way people behave here during the raids. How little do they think what others are going through! With us it's all over in a few minutes. I have now finished the memoirs from *The House of the Dead*, by Dostoievsky. It contains much that is brilliant and sound. I am pondering a good deal on his contention (by no means a passing phase) that man cannot live without hope, and men who are destitute of hope often become wild and wicked. It doesn't matter if that hope be an illusion. It's true that the importance of illusion in human life is not to be under-estimated, but for the Christian it is essential to have a hope which is based on solid foundations. However potent a force illusion may be, the influence of a sure and certain hope is infinitely greater, and the lives of those who possess it are invincible. 'Christ our hope'—this Pauline formula is our life's inspiration.

They have just come to fetch me for my exercise, but I'm finishing this letter to make sure it catches the post. Good-bye. I think of you every day. Your true and grateful friend. . . .

July 27th 1944

It takes a weight off the mind to have plenty to do, or so it would seem to me. Your summary of our theological theme is a model of lucidity and simplicity. The problem of natural religion is also that of unconscious Christianity, a subject with which I am more and more concerned. Lutheran dogmatics distinguishes between *fides directa* and *fides reflexa*, especially in connexion with infant baptism. I should not be at all surprised if we have put our finger on a very far-reaching problem here.

[172

. . . So you think the Bible has very little to say about health, fortune, vigour, etc. That is certainly not true of the Old Testament. The intermediate theological category between God and human fortune is, it seems to me, that of blessing. There is indeed no concern for fortune in the Old Testament, but there is a concern for the blessing of God, which includes all earthly blessings as well. In this blessing the whole of earthly life is claimed for God, and all his promises are included in it. It would be natural to suppose that as usual the New Testament spiritualizes the teaching of the Old at this point, and that therefore the Old Testament blessing is super-seded in the New. But surely it is hardly accidental that sick-ness and death are mentioned in connexion with the misuse of the Lord's Supper (the cup of blessing, I Corinthians 10.16: I Coronthians 11.30), or that Jesus is said to restore men to health, and that while his disciples were with him they are said to 'lack nothing'. Is it right therefore to set the Old Testament blessing against the cross? That is what Kierkegaard did; but the trouble is, it makes the cross, or suffering at any rate, an abstract principle. And this is just what gives rise to an unhealthy asceticism, and deprives suffering of its element of contingency upon a divine ordinance. It is true that in the Old Testament the recipient of a blessing has to endure much suffering into the bargain (e.g. Abraham, Isaac, Jacob and Joseph), but there is never any idea that fortune and suffering, blessing and cross are mutually exclusive and contradictory, any more than in the New Testament. The only difference between the two Testaments at this point is that in the Old the blessing also includes the cross, and in the New the cross also includes the blessing.

To turn to a different point, not only action, but also suffer-ing is a way to freedom. The deliverance consists in placing our cause unreservedly in the hands of God. Whether our deeds are wrought in faith or not depends on our realization that suffering is the extension of action and the perfection of freedom. That, to my mind, is very important and very comforting.

173]

I am getting on all right, and there's nothing to report about the family either. Hans[1] is definitely down with diphtheria, but there seems to be good hope for him. Good-bye, and keep up your spirits as we are doing. And don't forget—we *shall* meet again soon!

[1] Hans von Dohnanyi, also in prison since April 5th, 1943.

MISCELLANEOUS THOUGHTS

Giordano Bruno: 'There is something frightening about the sight of a friend: no enemy can be so terrifying as he.' What do you make of that? I am trying hard, but I really can't make head or tail of it. Is he thinking of the dangers inseparable from close intimacy, as in the case of Judas?
Spinoza: 'Emotion cannot be expelled by reason, but only by a stronger emotion.'

★　　★　　★

It is the characteristic excellence of the strong man that he can bring momentous issues to the fore and make a decision about them. The weak are always forced to decide between alternatives they have not chosen themselves.

★　　★　　★

We are so constituted that we always find perfection boring. Whether it has always been so I do not know. But it is the only way I can explain why I care so little for Raphael or Dante's *Paradise*. Similarly, I find everlasting ice or everlasting blue sky equally unattractive. I look for perfection in the human, the living and the earthly, and therefore neither in the Apolline nor the Dionysian nor the Faustian. I always prefer a moderate, temperate climate.

★　　★　　★

The transcendent is not infinitely remote, but close at hand.

★　　★　　★

Absolute seriousness is not without a dose of humour.

★　　★　　★

The essence of chastity is not the suppression of lust, but the total orientation of one's life towards a goal. Without such a goal, chastity is bound to become ridiculous. Chastity is the *sine qua non* of lucidity and concentration.

★　　★　　★

Death is the supreme festival on the road to freedom.

★　　★　　★

Please excuse these pompous pieces of wisdom. They are fragments of conversations that have never taken place, and to that extent they belong to you. When you are forced as I am to live entirely in your thoughts, the silliest things come to your mind:—I mean, jotting down the odd thoughts that come into your head.

August 3rd 1944

. . . I wonder whether you will be on the move again soon? And where to? I should like to know whether you have read my poems. You must read the very long one in rhyme, *Nächtliche Stimmen in Tegel.* I am enclosing the outline of a book I have planned. I don't know whether you will be able to make anything of it, but I believe you already have some idea what I am driving at. I only hope I shall be given the peace and strength to finish it. The Church must get out of her stagnation. We must move out again into the open air of intellectual discussion with the world, and risk shocking people if we are to cut any ice. I feel obliged to tackle this question myself as one who, though a 'modern' theologian, is still aware of the debt we owe to liberal theology. There will not be many of the younger men who combine both trends in themselves. What a lot I could do with your help! But even when we have talked things over and clarified our minds, we still need to pray, for it is only in the spirit of prayer that a work like this can be begun and carried through.

OUTLINE FOR A BOOK

I should like to write a book not more than 100 pages long, and with three chapters.

1. A Stocktaking of Christianity.
2. The Real Meaning of the Christian Faith.
3. Conclusions.

Chapter 1 to deal with:

(*a*) The coming of age of humanity (along the lines already suggested). The insuring of life against accident, ill-fortune. If elimination of danger impossible, at least its minimization. Insurance (which although it thrives upon accidents, seeks to mitigate their effects) a western phenomenon. The goal, to be independent of nature. Nature formerly conquered by spiritual means, with us by technical organization of various kinds. Our immediate environment not nature, as formerly, but organization. But this immunity produces a new crop of dangers, i.e. the very organization.

Consequently there is a need for spiritual vitality. What protection is there against the danger of organization? Man is once more faced with the problem of himself. He can cope with every danger except the danger of human nature itself. In the last resort it all turns upon man.

(*b*) The decay of religion in a world that has come of age. 'God' as a working hypothesis, as a stop-gap for our embarrassments, now superfluous (as already intimated).

(*c*) The Protestant Church. Pietism as the last attempt to maintain evangelical Christianity as a religion. Lutheran orthodoxy—the attempt to rescue the Church as an institution for salvation. The Confessing Church and the theology of revelation. A δὸς μοὶ ποῦ στῶ over against the world, involving a 'factual' interest in Christianity. Art and science seeking for a foundation. The over-all achievement of the Confessing Church: championing ecclesiastical interests, but little personal faith in Jesus Christ. 'Jesus' disappearing from sight. Sociologically, no effect on the masses—interest confined to the

upper and lower middle classes. Incubus of traditional vocabu-
lary, difficult to understand. The decisive factor: the Church
on the defensive. Unwillingness to take risks in the service of
humanity.

(*d*) Public morals—as evidenced by sexual behaviour.

Chapter 2
(*a*) 'Worldliness' and God.
(*b*) What do we mean by 'God'? Not in the first place an
abstract belief in his omnipotence, etc. That is not a genuine
experience of God, but a partial extension of the world.
Encounter with Jesus Christ, implying a complete orientation
of human being in the experience of Jesus as one whose only
concern is for others. This concern of Jesus for others the
experience of transcendence. This freedom from self, maintained to the point of death, the sole ground of his omnipotence, ominiscience and ubiquity. Faith is participation in this
Being of Jesus (incarnation, cross and resurrection). Our relation to God not a religious relationship to a supreme Being,
absolute in power and goodness, which is a spurious conception of transcendence, but a new life for others, through participation in the Being of God. The transcendence consists not
in tasks beyond our scope and power, but in the nearest thing
to hand. God in human form, not, as in other religions, in
animal form—the monstrous, chaotic, remote and terrifying—
nor yet in abstract form—the absolute, metaphysical, infinite,
etc.—nor yet in the Greek divine-human of autonomous man,
but man existing for others, and hence the Crucified. A life
based on the transcendent.

(*c*) This as the starting point for the reinterpretation of
biblical terminology. (Creation, fall, atonement, repentance,
faith, the new life, the last things.)

(*d*) Cultus. (Details to follow later, in particular on cultus
and religion.)

(*e*) What do we really believe? I mean, believe in such a way
as to stake our whole lives upon it? The problem of the
Apostles' Creed? 'What must I believe?' the wrong question.
Antiquated controversies, especially those between the different

confessions. The Lutheran *versus* Reformed, and to some extent, the Catholic *versus* Protestant controversy. These divisions may at any time be revived with passion, but they no longer carry real conviction. Impossible to prove this, but necessary to take the bull by the horns. All we can prove is that the faith of the Bible and Christianity does not stand or fall by these issues. Barth and the Confessing Church have encouraged us to entrench ourselves behind the 'faith of the Church', and evade the honest question, what is our real and personal belief? Hence lack of fresh air, even in the Confessing Church. To say, 'It's the Church's faith, not mine', can be a clericalist subterfuge, and outsiders always regard it as such. Much the same applies to the suggestion of the dialectical theologians that we have no control over our faith, and so it is impossible for us to say what we do believe. There may be a place for such considerations, but they do not release us from the duty of being honest with ourselves. We cannot, like the Catholics, identify ourselves *tout court* with the Church. (This incidentally explains the popular complaint about Catholic insincerity.) Well then, what do we really believe? Answer, see (*b*), (*c*) and (*d*).

Chapter 3
Consequences

The Church is her true self only when she exists for humanity. As a fresh start she should give away all her endowments to the poor and needy. The clergy should live solely on the free-will offerings of their congregations, or possibly engage in some secular calling. She must take her part in the social life of the world, not lording it over men, but helping and serving them. She must tell men, whatever their calling, what it means to live in Christ, to exist for others. And in particular, our own Church will have to take a strong line with the blasphemies of *hybris*, power-worship, envy and humbug, for these are the roots of evil. She will have to speak of moderation, purity, confidence, loyalty, steadfastness, patience, discipline, humility, content and modesty. She must not underestimate the importance of human example, which

[180

has its origin in the humanity of Jesus, and which is so important in the teaching of St. Paul. It is not abstract argument, but concrete example which gives her word emphasis and power. I hope to take up later this subject of example, and its place in the New Testament. It is something we have well-nigh forgotten. Further: the question of revising the creeds (the Apostles' Creed). Revision of Christian apologetics. Reform of the training for the ministry and the pattern of clerical life.

All this is very crude and sketchy, but there are certain things I want to say simply and clearly, things which we so often prefer to ignore. Whether I shall succeed or not is another matter, and I shall certainly find it difficult without your help. But I hope in this way to do something for the sake of the Church of the future.

August 10th 1944

I can well understand it when you say you are getting tired of living on memory. But gratitude is a force which constantly rekindles memory. It is just at such times as these that one should make a special point of thanksgiving in one's prayers. Above all, we should avoid getting absorbed in the present moment, and foster that peace of mind which springs from noble thoughts, measuring all other things by them. Alas, there are so few who are capable of it, and that is what makes it so hard to put up with our fellow human-beings. It is weakness rather than wickedness that degrades a man, and it needs profound sympathy to put up with that. But all the time God still reigns in heaven.

I am now working on those three chapters I told you about. You are quite right, intellectual discovery is one of the joys of life, and that is why I find this work of mine so enthralling. . . . To feel that one counts for something with other people is one of the joys of life. What matters here is not how many friends we have, but how deeply we are attached to them. After all, personal relationships count for more than anything else. That is why the 'successful man' of the modern world cuts so little ice—and the same goes for the demi-gods and lunatics who know nothing about personal relationships. God makes use of us in his dealings with other people. All else is closely akin to *hybris*. Of course it is possible to cultivate personal relationships and to try to mean something to other people in all too conscious a way, as I happened to discover recently in the letters of Gabriel von Bülow-Humboldt. It can lead to the cult of the 'human', which is a gross exaggeration. What I mean, however, is the simple fact that people are more important in life than anything else. Of course that does not mean that we should belittle the world of things or success in that sphere. But what is the best book or picture or house, or any property to me compared with my wife, my parents, or my friend? One can of course speak like that only if one has found others in one's life. For many to-day man is just a part of the world of things; the experience of the human simply

[182

eludes them. Fortunately for us, we have enjoyed this experience abundantly.

I have often noticed how much depends on stretching ourselves to the limit. Many people are spoilt by being satisfied with mediocrity. It may mean that they get to the top more quickly, for they have fewer inhibitions to overcome. I have found it one of the most potent educative factors in our family that we have had so many inhibitions to overcome (I mean, such obstacles as lack of relevance, clarity, naturalness, tact, simplicity, etc.) before we can speak freely of what is in our minds. I believe you found it so with us at first. It often takes a long time to leap over such hurdles as these, and one often feels one could have achieved success with greater ease and less cost if these obstacles could have been avoided. . . . God does not give us everything we want, but he does fulfil his promises, i.e. he still remains Lord of the earth and still preserves his Church, constantly renewing our faith and not laying on us more than we can bear, gladdening us with his nearness and help, hearing our prayers and leading us along the best and straightest road to himself. In this way, God creates in us praise for himself.

August 21st 1944

Once more I have taken up the texts (Numbers 11.23: II Corinthians 1.20) and meditated upon them for a space. The key to everything is the 'in him'. All that we rightly expect from God and pray for is to be found in Jesus Christ. The God of Jesus Christ has nothing to do with all that we, in our human way, think he can and ought to do. We must persevere in quiet meditation on the life, sayings, deeds, sufferings and death of Jesus in order to learn what God promises and what he fulfils. One thing is certain: we must always live close to the presence of God, for that is newness of life; and then nothing is impossible for all things are possible with God; no earthly power can touch us without his will, and danger can only drive us closer to him. We can claim nothing for ourselves, and yet we may pray for everything. Our joy is hidden

183]

in suffering, our life in death. But all through we are sustained in a wondrous fellowship. To all this God in Jesus has given his Yea and his Amen, and that is the firm ground on which we stand. In these turbulent times we are always forgetting what it is that makes life really worth while. We think that life has a meaning for us so long as such and such a person still lives. But the truth is that if this earth was good enough for the Man Jesus Christ, if a man like him really lived in it, then, and only then, has life a meaning for us. If Jesus had not lived, then our life, in spite of all the other people we know and honour and love, would be without meaning. No doubt we often forget in such times as these the meaning and purpose of our profession. But is not this the simplest way of putting it? The word 'meaning' does occur in the Bible, but it is only a translation of what the Bible means by 'promise'.

I am conscious of the inadequacy of these words to express my meaning and intention, which is to give you steadfastness and joy and certainty in your loneliness. This day of loneliness need not be a lost day, if it helps you to see more clearly the convictions on which you are going to build your life in time to come. I have often found it a help to spend some time in the evening thinking of those who I know are remembering me in their prayers, both children and grown-ups. I believe I owe it to the prayers of others, both known and unknown, that I have been so often preserved in safety.

Now another point: we are often told in the New Testament to 'be strong' (I Corinthians 16.13: Ephesians 6.10: II Timothy 2.1: I John 2.14). Is not the weakness of men often more dangerous than deliberate malice? I mean, such things as stupidity, lack of independence, forgetfulness, laziness, idleness, corruption, being easily led astray, etc. Christ does not only make men good: he makes them strong too. The sins of weakness are the real human sins, the deliberate sins are diabolical, and no doubt strong as well! I must ponder further on this. Good-bye: take care of yourself, and don't give up hope!

August 23rd 1944

Please don't ever get anxious or worried about me, but
don't forget to pray for me—I'm sure you don't! I am so sure
of God's guiding hand, and I hope I shall never lose that
certainty. You must never doubt that I am travelling my
appointed road with gratitude and cheerfulness. My past life
is replete with God's goodness, and my sins are covered by the
forgiving love of Christ crucified. I am thankful for all those
who have crossed my path, and all I wish is never to cause
them sorrow, and that they like me will always be thankful
for the forgiveness and mercy of God and sure of it. Please don't
for a moment get upset by all this, but let it rejoice your heart.
But I did want to say this for once, and I could not think of
anyone else who would take it in the right spirit.

Did you get the poem on freedom? I'm afraid it was very
unpolished, but it's a subject about which I feel deeply.

I am now working on the chapter about 'Taking Stock of
Christianity'. I'm afraid I can't work unless I smoke pretty
hard, though I have many sources of supply, thank goodness,
so I manage all right. I am often shocked at the things I am
saying, especially in the first part, which is mainly critical. I
shall be glad when I get to the more positive part. But the
whole subject has never been properly thrashed out, so it
sounds very undigested. However, it can't be printed at present
anyhow, and it will doubtless improve with waiting. I find it
hard going having to write everything by hand, and I can
scarcely read what I have written. Amusingly enough, I am
obliged to use German handwriting, and then there are all the
corrections. Perhaps I shall be able to make a fair copy. . . .

I do so hope you will have a quiet time both in body and
mind. May God take care of you, and all of us, and grant us
the joy of meeting again soon! I am praying for you every day!

Your true and grateful friend,

D.

VI
Signs of Life
from the Prinz Albert Strasse

December 28th 1944

Dear Mama,

I am so glad I have just got permission to write you a birthday letter. Rather a hurried one, I'm afraid, for the post is just going. All I want is to do something to brighten up these troublous days for you. Dear Mama, I want you and Papa to know that you are constantly in my thoughts, and that I thank God for all you have been to me and the rest of the family. I know you have always lived for us, and have never had a life of your own. And that is why there is no one else with whom I can share all that I am going through. . . . Thank you for all the love you have brought into my cell during the past year: it has made every day easier to bear. I believe these years, hard as they have been, will have bound us more closely together. My New Year's wish for you and papa, and indeed for all of us, is that it may bring us at least an occasional glimpse of light, and that we may have the joy of reunion some day. May God keep you both well. With loving wishes, dear, dear Mother, for a happy birthday.

Your grateful
Dietrich

NEW YEAR
(1945)

With every power for good to stay and guide me,
comforted and inspired beyond all fear,
I'll live these days with you in thought beside me,
and pass, with you, into the coming year.

The old year still torments our hearts, unhastening:
the long days of our sorrow still endure:
Father, grant to the souls thou hast been chastening
that thou hast promised, the healing and the cure.

Should it be ours to drain the cup of grieving
even to the dregs of pain, at thy command,
we will not falter, thankfully receiving
all that is given by thy loving hand.

But, should it be thy will once more to release us
to life's enjoyment and its good sunshine,
that which we've learned from sorrow shall increase us,
and all our life be dedicate as thine.

To-day, let candles shed their radiant greeting:
lo, on our darkness are they not thy light
leading us, haply, to our longed-for meeting?—
Thou canst illumine even our darkest night.

When now the silence deepens for our harkening
grant we may hear thy children's voices raise
from all the unseen world around us darkening
their universal pæan, in thy praise.

While all the powers of Good aid and attend us
boldly we'll face the future, be it what may.
At even, and at morn, God will befriend us,
and oh, most surely on each new year's day!

January 17th 1945

Dear Parents,

. . . The last two years have taught me how little we can get along with. But every day thousands are losing all they have, and when we remember that, we know that we have no right to call anything our own.

Is H. W. really flying in the East? and R.'s husband? Many thanks for your letter. I read all my letters through until I know them by heart. Now a few requests. I was disappointed not to receive any books to-day. Commissar Sonderegger would quite willingly accept them every now and then, and I would be most grateful. Also there were no matches, face cloths or towel this time. Pardon my mentioning the subject; otherwise everything was wonderful. Could I please have some tooth paste and a few coffee beans? And, dear Papa, could you get me from the library *Lienhard* and *Abendstunden eines Einsiedlers* by H. Pestalozzi, *Sozialpädagogik*, by P. Natorp, and *Lives of Great Men* by Plutarch?

I am getting on all right. Take care of yourselves. Once more, thank you for everything.

With fondest love,
Your grateful
Dietrich

Index of Biblical References